Psychic Photography

Psychic Photography

Threshold of a New Science?

Hans Holzer

McGraw-Hill Book Company

New York   San Francisco   Toronto

PSYCHIC PHOTOGRAPHY

Library of Congress Catalog Card Number: 68–55269
FIRST EDITION 29663

Contents

Introduction

Psychic photography, in all its manifestations, is but one segment of the total spectrum of psychic phenomena. Over the past one hundred-odd years, researchers and authors have traditionally divided psychic phenomena into two broad categories: *mental* and *physical*. Among the manifestations of mental psychism are telepathy, clairvoyance, precognition, et cetera—phenomena in which there is no concurrent or residual physical evidence of any paranormal occurence.° The category of physical psychism includes the phenomena of poltergeists, levitation, precipitation, apports, materialization, et cetera, in which concurrent or residual physical evidence is present. The psychic photographs apparently produced under controlled conditions and reported within this book belong in the latter category. The production of psychic photographs, however, seems to be a mental/physical phenomenon of a paranormal character which manifests in the presence of one or more individuals who are termed to be "psychic," by virtue of the fact that such phenomena appear to be associated with them. Thus it is similar to the various forms of automatism—automatic writing, painting, and so forth; dowsing, or speaking in tongues; and certain instances of phenomena associated with the laying-on-of-hands.

The great significance of this last category of psychical phenomena lies in its manifestation and the residual record of tangible, measurable, physical effects. It fulfills in large measure the skeptic's oft-repeated demand for evidence that can be "seen and felt." While psychic-photographic phenomena do not yet constitute, totally, the ideal "repeatable scientific experiment," they do represent an approach to that ideal sufficient to challenge the hard-core skeptic, layman or scientist, to make the next move. Here are apparently paranormal phenomena, measurable and recordable—now what to do with them? Does the scientific "establishment" continue to deny their existence, or does it undertake their responsible investigation?

This question summarizes the importance of Mr. Holzer's work and of this book in particular. The photographs here contained, and the conditions under which they are reported to have come into existence, admit of only two possible conclusions:

a. Mr. Holzer is an outright fraud, in which case he should be exposed;

or

b. the phenomena and the results are as he represents them and deserve to be accepted as such, in which case those who would challenge their authenticity have the duty, to themselves and society, to investigate and publicly report their findings.

For those who think seriously about the evidence this book contains, and its relation-

° That is, phenomena which cannot be explained in terms of present scientific knowledge.

ship to scientific knowledge, note should be taken of the distinction between two types of data on which scientific knowledge is built. Concepts and facts of data derived from laboratory experiments are generally understood and accepted by scientists and laymen alike. In the collection of such data, much emphasis is placed on the design of the experiment, which is under the control of the experimenter. On the other hand, data which occur spontaneously, or in nature, are observed as they occur and under the conditions of occurrence.

Information collected under these latter conditions is equally valid, scientifically, to the extent that it is responsibly observed; that is, to the extent that observations are made and validated according to the best concepts and practices of scientific observation, and the natural conditions under which the phenomena manifested are documented. Darwin's conclusions were based on his observations of natural phenomena—not laboratory studies. Much of our knowledge of the Universe comes from scientific observation of naturally occurring celestial phenomena—not studies conducted in the laboratory. So, too, the scientific study of volcanoes, earthquakes, hurricanes, et cetera, are primarily conducted by scientific observation of the phenomena as they occur naturally, and the record of their existence which they leave behind.

Mr. Holzer's investigations into naturally occurring psychical phenomena, in many areas of the world, his intimate knowledge and association with the world's foremost "psychics," and his breadth of historical and philosophical scholarship qualify him as a competent reporter in this field. Admittedly his interests have commercial overtones—his style tends, at times, to be flamboyant. This is understandable; he is a professional writer and lecturer, and frequently appears on television to discuss these subjects. Admittedly he does not qualify as a scientist in terms of his formal education (he was trained as a historian), nor is he likely to be accepted as such by scientists, primarily, I suspect, because of the nature of his data. It would appear, however, that Mr. Holzer has responsibly collected and documented evidence of naturally occurring phenomena which are not explainable within the context of present scientific knowledge. This book dramatizes that such apparently paranormal phenomena can lend themselves to objective scientific study, without reference to any metaphysical or religious considerations. Practically speaking, the only avenues of expression currently open to Mr. Holzer and other researchers into these matters are the journals of societies and organizations devoted to the field (i.e., "believers"), or the popular public media of books, magazines, radio, and television.

If history can be relied upon as a guide to future probabilities, one can expect, and hope, that the publication of these photographs and of the many other responsible reports of paranormal phenomena will eventually develop such a pressure of popular awareness, of interest and intellectual demand for answers, that the scientific establishment will find it appropriate, legitimate and respectable to investigate such phenomena and to report their findings in recognized scientific journals.

Until psychism is regarded as a legitimate area of scientific inquiry we must rely upon, and be indebted to, those private individuals, publishers and broadcasters who have the courage to bring psychic phenomena to public attention. In the face of the evidence contained in this book, the research results reported by many other responsible investigators over the years, and my personal observations, it is my opinion that the modern scientist or layman who rejects the existence or even the possibility of psychical phenomena without first seriously reviewing the evidence is guilty of an attitude more appropriate to the Middle Ages than to today. He places himself, intellectually and professionally, in the company of those who ridiculed and persecuted Copernicus, Galileo, and Columbus.

Prof. Robert J. Jeffries,
University of Bridgeport

The "Track Record" of Psychic Photography

Ever since man first wondered about a life after death, he has tried to find some convincing proof, or at least evidence, that there is something within us all that survives the death of the physical body.

For the past one hundred years, psychic research has painstakingly assembled proof for the continuance of life and has gradually emerged from a metaphysical mantle into the full glare of scientific inquiry. Although various researchers interpret the results of these investigations according to their own attitudes toward survival of human personality, it is no longer possible to bury the evidence itself, as some materialistically inclined scientists in other fields have attempted to do over the years. The challenge is always present: does man have a soul, scientifically speaking, and if so, how can we prove it?

Material on communications with the so-called dead is very large and, to me, often convincing, though not necessarily all of it in the way it is sometimes presented by partisans of the spiritualist religion. But additional proof that man does continue an existence in what Dr. Joseph Rhine, then of Duke University, has called "the world of the mind" was always wanted, especially the kind of proof that could be viewed objectively without the need for subjective observation through psychic experiences, either spontaneous or induced in the laboratory. One of the greatest potential tools was given man when photography was in-vented: for if we could photograph the dead under conditions that carefully exclude trick-ery, we would surely be so much the wiser—and the argument for survival would indeed be stronger.

Photography itself goes back to the 1840s, when the technique evolved gradually from very crude light-and-shadow pictures, through daguerreotypes and tintypes to photography as we now know it.

Major Tom Patterson, a British psychic re-searcher, in a recent booklet entitled *Spirit Photography,* has dealt with the beginnings of photographic mediumship in Britain, where it has produced the largest amount of experi-mental material in the century since.

But the initial experiment took place in 1862, in Boston, not Britain, twenty-three years after photography itself came into being. William H. Mumler, an engraver, who was neither interested in nor a believer in spiritu-alism or any other form of psychic research, had been busy in his off hours experimenting with a camera. At that time the photographic camera was still a novelty. The engraver liked to take snapshots of his family and friends to learn more about his camera. Imagine Mr. Mumler's surprise and dismay when some of his negatives showed faces that were not sup-posed to be on them. In addition to the living people he had so carefully posed and photo-graphed, Mumler discovered the portraits of dead relatives alongside the "normal" portraits.

This was the beginning of psychic photography. It happened accidentally—if there is such a thing as an accident in our well-organized universe—and the news of Mumler's unsought achievements spread across the world. Other photographers, both professionals and amateurs, discovered talents similar to Mumler's, and the psychic research societies in Britain and America began to take notice of this amazing development.

Since then a great many changes have taken place in our technology and we have greater knowledge of its pitfalls. But the basic principle of photography is still the same. A film covered with silver salts is exposed to the radiation called light and reacts to it. This reaction results in certain areas of the emulsion being eaten away, leaving an exact replica of the image seen by the camera lens on the photographic film. Depending on the intensity with which light hits the various portions of the film, the eating away of silver salts will vary, thus rendering the tones and shadings of the resulting negative upon light-sensitive photographic paper and hence the positive print, which is a mechanical reproduction of the negative's light and shadow areas, but in reverse.

To make a print, the operator merely inserts his finished negative into a printer, places the light-sensitive paper underneath the negative and exposes it through the negative with an electric light. Nothing new can be added in this manner, nor can anything already on the negative be taken away, but the skill of the craftsman operating the printer will determine how well balanced the resulting positive print will be, depending on the duration and intensity of the printing lamp.

Most people who are photographers know these simple facts, but there are many who are not, and for whom this information might be useful.

The obtaining of any sort of images on photographic paper, especially recognizable pictures such as faces or figures, without having first made a negative in the usual manner is, of course, a scientific impossibility—*except* in psychic photography.

Until the arrival on the scene of Polaroid cameras and Polaroid film, this was certainly 100 per cent true. The Polaroid method, with its instant result and development of film within a matter of a few seconds after exposure, adds the valuable element of close supervision to an experiment. It also allows an even more direct contact between psychic radiation and sensitive surface. The disadvantage of Polaroid photography is its ephemeral character. Even the improved film does not promise to stay unspoiled forever, and it is wise to protect unusual Polaroid photographs by obtaining slide copies. Actually, Polaroid photography uses a combination of both film and sensitive paper simultaneously, one being peeled off the other after the instant development process inside the camera.

Fakery with the ordinary type of photography would depend on double exposure or double printing by unscrupulous operators, in which case no authentic negative could be produced that would stand up to *experienced* scrutiny. Fakery with Polaroid equipment is impossible if camera, film and operator are closely watched. Because of the great light sensitivity of Polaroid film, double exposure, if intended, is not a simple matter, as one exposure would severely cancel out the other and certainly leave traces of double exposure. And the film, of course, would have to be switched in the presence of the observer, something not even a trained conjurer is likely to do to an experienced psychic investigator. A psychic researcher must also be familiar with magic and sleight-of-hand tricks, in order to qualify for that title.

The important thing to remember about psychic photography is that the bulk of it occurred unexpectedly and often embarrassingly to amateur photographers not the least bit interested in parapsychology or any form of occultism. The extras on the negatives were not placed there by these people to confuse themselves. They were the portraits of dead relatives or friends that could be recognized. The literature on this phase of psychic photography, notably in Britain, is impressive; and I particularly recommend the scholarly work by F. W. Warrick, the celebrated British parapsychologist, called *Experiments in Psychics,* in which

hundreds of experimental photographs are reproduced. Mr. Warrick's work concerns itself primarily with the photographic mediumship of Mrs. Emma Deane, although other examples are included. It was published in 1939 by E. P. Dutton. Mr. Warrick points out that he and his colleagues, having spent some thirty years working with and closely supervising their subjects, knew their personal habits and quirks. Any kind of trickery was therefore out of the question, unless one wanted to call a researcher who propounded unusual ideas self-deluded or incompetent, as some latter-day critics have done to Harry Price and Sir William Crookes, respected British psychic researchers now dead.

Any person who is not present when the original experiments or investigations take place and who does not possess firsthand knowledge of the conditions and processes of that investigation is no more qualified to judge its results than an armchair strategist trying to rewrite history. Although Major Patterson's booklet frankly uses the scientific evidence at hand to support the spiritualistic view, it also serves as a useful source of factual information. Mumler's record as the "first" spirit photographer is upheld by U.S. Court of Appeals Judge John Edmond, who investigated Mumler personally and obtained photographs under test conditions of people known only to him who were dead. Originally, Judge Edmond had gone into the investigation thinking it was all a deception. In a letter published by the *New York Herald* on August 6, 1853, however, the judge spoke not only of Mumler's experiments but also of his subsequent sittings with well-known mediums of his day. These investigations had convinced him that spiritualism had a valid base, and he became a confirmed believer from then on in, displaying some psychic abilities of his own as time went by.

In England, the craft of psychic photography developed slowly from the 1879s onward. The first man in Britain to show successful results in this field was a man named Frederick Hudson, who in 1872 produced a number of authentic likenesses of the dead under conditions excluding fraud. Several experiments were undertaken under the careful scrutiny of Dr. Alfred Russel Wallace, a famed naturalist in his day. Dr. Wallace attested to the genuineness of the observed phenomena. Since then several dozen talented psychic photographers have appeared upon the scene, producing for a few pennies genuine likenesses of persons known to have died previously in the presence of "sitters" (or portrait subjects) they had never before met in their lives.

As the craft became better known and men of science wondered about it, researchers devised more and more rigid test conditions for this type of experimental psychic photography. Film, paper, cameras, developing fluid—in short, all implements necessary to produce photographs of any kind—were furnished, con-trolled and held by uncommitted researchers; the medium was not allowed to touch anything and was kept at a distance from the camera and film. In many cases he was not even present in the room itself. Nevertheless psychic "extras" kept appearing on the properly exposed film and were duly recognized as the portraits of dead persons, often of obscure identity, but traceable as relatives or friends of someone present. Occasionally, as with John Myers, now America's leading psychic photographer, in his early days the portraits thus obtained by the photographic medium were strangers to all concerned until the pictures were first published in *Psychic News,* a leading spiritualist newspaper of the day; only then did the "owners" of the psychic "extras" write in to the editor to claim their dead relatives!

Despite the overwhelming evidence that these photographs were genuine—in almost all cases even the motive for fraud was totally absent—some researchers kept rejecting then—and indeed they do now—the possibility that the results were anything but fraudulently manufactured double exposures. Even so brilliant a person as Eileen Garrett, president of Parapsychology Foundation, insisted for many years that all psychic photographs *had* to be fraudulent, having been so informed by a pair of self-styled experts. It was only when I myself produced the photographs of ghosts herein published, and acquainted Mrs. Garrett with the camera, film and other details of how the pictures were obtained, that she reluctantly agreed with me that we had indeed "made a breakthrough" in the field of psychic photography. Prejudice against anything involving a major shift in one's thinking, philosophy of life and general training is much stronger than we dare admit to ourselves sometimes.

Often psychic photography also occurs at so-called home circles where neither money nor notoriety is involved and where certainly no need exists for self-delusion by those taking the pictures. They are, presumably, already convinced of survival of personality after death, otherwise they would not be members of the circle.

Photographs of ghosts or haunted areas are much rarer because of the great element of chance in obtaining any results at all. Whereas psychic photography in the experimental sense is subject to schedules and human plans, the taking of ghost pictures is not. Even I had neither advance knowledge nor control over the ones I managed to obtain, and I could not do it again that way if I tried.

We still don't know *all* of the conditions that make these extraordinary photographs possible and, until we do, obtaining them will be a hit-and-miss affair at best. But the fact that genuine photographs of what are commonly called ghosts have been taken by a number of people, under conditions excluding fraud or faulty equipment, of course, is food for serious thought.

An example in recent years is the photograph of a Danish sailor fighting for his life at Ballyheigue Castle, Ireland, taken by a vacationing army officer named Captain P. D. O'Donnell, on June 4, 1962. Unbeknownst to Captain O'Donnell, that was the anniversary of the sailor's death during the so-called "silver raid," in which the silver stored at the castle was stolen by local bandits and fighting ensued. Captain O'Donnell took this snapshot without thought or knowledge of ghosts, while inspecting the ruins of the once proud castle. The picture was later lost in transit and could not be located by the post office. The captain, a professional officer and a practical man, did not pay too much attention to what to him was a puzzling fact and nothing more.

Many newspapers the world over, including *The People* of July 3, 1966, reported and published a ghost photograph taken by eighteen-year-old Gordon Carroll, a clerk, of Northampton, England, in St. Mary the Virgin Church, Woodford, Northhamptonshire. The picture clearly shows a monk kneeling before the altar, but at the time he took it Gordon was the only person inside the church. Fortunately, he found an understanding ear in the person of Canon John Pearce-Higgins, Provost of Southwark Cathedral and a member of the Church's Fellowship of Psychical and Physical Research. Mr. Pearce-Higgins, after inspecting camera and film and questioning the young man, was satisfied that the phenomenon was authentic. Gordon used a tripod and a brand-new Ilford Sportsman Rangefinder camera. He loaded it with Agfa C.T.18 film, which he often uses to photograph stained-glass windows in churches, a hobby of his. The Agfa Company, on examining the film, confirmed that trick photography had not been used and that neither film nor developing showed any faults. As for the ghost, no one seems to have bothered to find out who he was. The church itself is a very ancient place, mentioned in the *Domesday Book*, a list of important properties compiled under William the Conqueror. A church stood on that spot even before the Norman conquest of Britain, so it is quite possible that at one time or other a monk died there, tragically becoming the ghost that Gordon's camera accidentally saw and recorded.

Joe Hyams, writer husband of actress Elke Sommer, has shared a haunted house with her for some time in Hollywood, only to give up to the ghost in the end. During the last stages of their occupancy, a photographer named Allan Grant, strictly a nonbeliever, took some pictures in the aftermath of a fire of mysterious origin. The pictures, published in *The Saturday Evening Post* of June 3, 1967, clearly show manifestations not compatible with ordinary photographic results. At this writing I have promised the Hyamses to have a go at what still is a haunted house, since none of the assorted clairvoyants, mystics et al. have been able or qualified to get to the heart of the matter—or ghost.

The very latest development in the area of psychic photography, although not concerned with images of ghosts, is still germane to the entire question. Thought forms registering on photographic film or other light-sensitive surfaces are the result of years of hard work by Colorado University's Professor Jule Eisenbud, a well-known psychiatrist interested in parapsychology as well, with the Chicago photographic medium, Ted Serios. These amazing pictures have been recently published by Eisenbud in an impressive volume called *The World of Ted Serios*. In addition, more material has become available as the experiments continued and are indeed continuing today, thanks to the efforts of a number of universities and study groups who have belatedly recognized the importance of this type of experiment.

Serios has the ability of projecting images onto film or a TV tube of objects and scenes often at great distances in space, or even *time*. This includes places he has never visited or seen before. Dr. Eisenbud does not suggest that there are spirit forces at work here. He merely points out, quite rightly, that we do not as yet realize some of the areas in which the human mind can operate. Without having been present at the many sessions in which Eisenbud and a host of other scientists subjected Serios to every conceivable test, I cannot judge the results. But it appears to me from what I have read in the book, and from other Serios photographs shown to me privately, that Serios is capable of what we call astral projection. In these out-of-the-body states he does visit distant places in a flash, then almost instantly returns to his physical body and records the impressions received by his etheric eyes onto Polaroid film. Above all, I feel that Ted Serios is one of an impressive line of photography mediums.

There may be differences of opinion concerning the implications of psychic photography, with some quarters taking the attitude that it merely represents a record of past events that somehow got left behind in the atmosphere during the event itself. This is undoubtedly possible in a number of cases. But there are also an impressive number of other instances where this view does not fit and where only the unpopular theory (scientifically speaking) of survival of human personality in a thought world will satisfy as an explanation. Either way, psychic photography, like it or not, is the very threshold of a new science.

Experimental Psychic Photographs

The *possibility* of fraud is always present when planned experiments take place. But the possibility of an explosion is also always present when munitions are being manufactured, and nobody stops making them. One simply proceeds with great care in both cases. Magicians and other conjurers have, almost to a man, assaulted psychic photography as patently fake, since *they* could fake it. This, of course, is a neat trick. By suggesting the possibility as the probability, these limited individuals (spiritually speaking) miss the point of scientifically controlled experiments in psychic photography: it is not what *could* be that matters, but what actually *does* happen.

I have no valid reason to doubt the majority of the older psychic photographs I have examined but, since I was not present when they were taken and have no way of knowing how rigid the controls were at the time, I will not personally vouch for them. This does not mean that they are not genuine. It does mean that anything I vouch for has occurred in my presence and/or under my controls and with persons known to me under conditions generally considered appropriate by professional parapsychologists. When I studied the literature on this subject, notably Warrick's work on *Experiments in Psychics*, I was impressed by the sincerity of Warrick's approach and by his sensible controls through which he made sure that his subjects could not obtain their amazing results by trickery of any kind. Warrick's work

deals to a large extent with the mediumship of Mrs. Deane, a British psychic famed for her ability to produce photographs of the dead under conditions excluding fraud. It was the same Mrs. Deane who was once visited by John Myers, then a novice in the field. He came merely to have a "sitting," like everybody else who sought out the elderly lady, and, for a few pennies, was photographed in her presence. Frequently he was to discover afterward the portrait of a dead loved one near him on the plate! To Myers' surprise, Mrs. Deane told him that some day soon he would be taking her place. Myers smiled incredulously and walked out. But when Mrs. Deane's health failed some time later, Myers, who had since discovered his own psychic and photographic powers, did indeed take over her studio.

I met John Myers in New York in 1961 because I had heard of his special psychic talents and was anxious to test him. Myers, at that point, and more so now, was a man of independent means, a successful industrialist and well-known philanthropist who could not possibly gain anything from exposing himself to psychic research. But he also felt he owed something to his benefactors on "the other side of life," as the spiritualists call it, and for that reason he agreed to meet me. This indebtedness went back many years to when he was a dental surgeon in London, already aware of his psychic abilities and practicing two of his special crafts as sidelines. These were psychic photography—later a full-time occupation—and psychic healing. As a healer, he managed to help a wealthy American regain his eyesight where orthodox doctors had failed. In gratitude this man offered him a position in his company in New York. At the time John Myers was not making too much money, since he charged only a few pennies for each psychic photograph he took, and nothing for his healing work. He felt that the opportunity to go to America was being sent his way so that he might be useful in his new career *and* as a psychic, so he accepted.

In New York Myers proved himself a good asset to the company and eventually he rose to become its vice president, second only to the head of the company. Because of his new duties Myers now pursued his psychic work on only a sporadic basis, but behind the scenes he often backed other psychics or sponsored spiritualistic meetings that could not have found a hall were it not for Myers' financial support. He himself continued his activities as a psychic healer, however. Occasionally Myers agreed to tests, but only when important scientists or newspapermen were to be present. What Myers could no longer do in amount of work he made up for by the sheer power of observers' rosters.

I was able to test Myers' abilities as a psychic photographer on several occasions, under conditions I will presently describe. At no time did he try to influence me in any way, or suggest anything, except that he was and is a sensitive man who resents being insulted. On one occasion I managed to persuade him to give a second public demonstration of his psychic photography on television. Since the first TV test in 1961 was, to my mind, very impressive, I felt another such test might prove valuable also. The program that had requested this test was the American Broadcasting Company's late night show emceed by Les Crane. This brash young man had on a previous occasion proved himself to me to be a man without sympathy toward psychic research, but I was there to protect Myers from any unpleasant remarks. We had brought the usual chemicals, all open to examination, and the program's producer had provided the photographic paper to be exposed; that is, they had it ready. But the moment never came. They had booked too many "acts" on this particular occasion, so that time ran out before Myers and I could undertake the test. For over two hours Myers sat waiting quietly in the wings. But the little people who were in charge failed to understand the significance of Myers' willingness to do this experiment, and so he went home angry, quite rightly, and I haven't been able to coax him onto television since. Here, then, are the exact circumstances of my experiments with John Myers.

My first meeting with Myers in 1959 was followed by a sitting which was arranged for the purpose of demonstrating his abilities as a psychic photographer. This was in late July, and I set up the following test conditions: Myers was to accompany me on the afternoon of the planned sitting to a photographic supply store of my choice and selection, where I would select and purchase the light-sensitive paper he required. Myers asked the clerk for ordinary developing paper. There are many types, of varying light-sensitivity, and Myers picked a medium-fast paper. The clerk brought the package of paper and I satisfied myself that it was from a fresh batch of materials, properly sealed and in no way damaged or tampered with. I then placed my signature across all corners of the outer envelope, and Myers did the same. The reason for Myers' insistence that he too should be allowed to place his own safeguards on the package goes back many years. When still a young man in England gaining a reputation as a psychic photographer, Myers was challenged to a test by a brash young journalist named Lord Donegal. Not content to look for possible fraud by Myers, Donegal wanted to make sure he *would* be able to find some. Rather than take his chance that Myers might be honest, Donegal switched plates on him and thus produced a foolproof "fraud"— marked plates he himself had supplied. Naturally, Myers was accused publicly, and it took years of hard work to undo the damage. In the end, tiring of the joke, Donegal admitted his deeds. But the whole sorry business had

turned Myers from a friendly, openhearted man into a cautious, suspicious person, who never quite trusted any experimenter fully.

For this reason, Myers wanted his signature on the package next to mine, so that he too could be sure I had not been tampering with the package to his detriment. As soon as the bill for the paper was paid, I took the package and put it safely into my pocket. At no time did Myers hold it in his hands. We parted company and I went home, the package still in my possession. After dinner I went to Myers' apartment on Sutton Place, where he and five other witnesses were already present. One of these was a photographer named Hagedorn, a skeptic, and one was Myers' legal advisor, Jacob Gerstein, an attorney well known in business circles for his integrity and keen observation. Also present was the late Danton Walker, Broadway columnist of the *Daily News,* himself psychic and keenly interested in the subject, but by no means sure of its implications. None of the observers were "believers" as the term is usually used, but rather all were enlightened witnesses who were willing to accept unusual facts if they could be proven to them.

We repaired to a medium-sized room in which there was a table surrounded by four chairs, with additional chairs in the four corners. The only illumination came from a yellow overhead bulb, but the light was strong enough to read by without difficulty. The cor-

1. *a. Posthumous portrait of Holzer's mother obtained on television through mediumship of John Myers. Photograph taken during her lifetime is at right.*

b. Portrait of Holzer's aunt, killed during World War II, and her psychic picture.

c. Psychic picture of Holzer's friend Myers never saw.

HOW THIS PICTURE WAS OBTAINED.

Time: *September, 1961, 8 P.M.*

Place: *On the air, during a television program entitled* PM East *for Channel 5, New York, Mike Wallace, moderator.*

Light conditions: *Total darkness in the studio except for one overhead 60-watt yellow bulb, at a distance of about twenty inches.*

Camera: *No camera used.*

Film: *No film, but ordinary photographic printing paper (so-called gaslight paper), purchased independently by Mike Wallace at a shop of his own selection and kept sealed until air time.*

Exposure: *Immediately upon opening package of unexposed photographic paper, each sheet was immersed in developer individually by Wallace, then transferred by him to hypo for fixation of obtained images. At no time did medium John Myers or I touch photographic papers until after they had been covered by various impressions which could not be accounted for by ordinary means of exposure. Each sheet was exposed to yellow light for the short time it took the hands of Mike Wallace to move the sheet from the package to the liquid.*

Operator: *Mike Wallace, in the presence of myself and to my left, photographic medium John Myers, a dental surgeon and industrialist from London.*

1. *a.*

b.

c.

ners of the room were somewhat darker. Myers sat down on a chair in the left-hand corner, placed his hands over his eyes and went into trance. I took the photographic paper out of my pocket, where it had been all this time, and placed it on the table in plain view of everyone present. At no time had Myers or anyone else among the guests "brushed past" me, or jostled me—a typical means of switching packages. Whenever I have the misfortune of sharing a microphone with a professional conjurer, this is one of his "explanations" of how the psychic phenomena must have been accomplished. I am of course familiar with many tricks of magic and always look out for them, but nothing of the sort was attempted. The package was still sealed, exactly as it had been all afternoon. After about five minutes Myers breathed deeply and opened his eyes, saying with a somewhat tired voice, "The paper is now exposed. You can open the package." With that, Walker and I proceeded to tear open the outer envelope, then the package of light-sensitive paper itself, and quickly threw the twenty sheets contained in it into the developing liquid we had also brought along. As soon as the sheets hit the liquid, various things happened to them that really shouldn't have, if this had not been a psychic experiment.

Unexposed photographic paper should show uniform results when exposed to a 60-watt yellow light and then developed. But here we had different things happen with each and every sheet! Some were totally blank. Others had

2. a. b. c. Holzer supervising experiment of John Myers' psychic photography.

a. Pans for developer and fixative.

b. Holzer opening bag of chemicals.

c. Mr. and Mrs. Hans Holzer fascinated by results in pans.

2. *a.*

b.

c.

forms on them, and some showed human faces. A few showed symbols, such as a tombstone, a tablet, a cross. As rapidly as we could we worked over the whole pack. Walker pulled out the sheets and threw them into the developer. I pulled them from the latter and into the fixative solution and out into clear water. Myers was still on his chair in the corner. We then put all the papers on a big towel to dry, and turned on all the lights in the room. Without touching any of the prints, we started to examine the results of John Myers' psychic mediumship.

Clearly, if faces or figures appeared on these papers, fraud could not be the cause. One of the intriguing aspects of such an experiment is to hope for a likeness of someone one knew in physical life. Of course you never know *who* might turn up. Those who experiment or investigate psychic channels of various kinds, and anxiously hope for a specific loved one to make an entrance, are almost invariably disappointed. The genuine result of these experiments is quite unpredictable, as well it should be. So it was with considerable glee that I discovered among the faces a familiar one. As soon as the paper was completely dry I took it over to a strong light to make sure I was not guilty of wishful thinking. No, there was no mistake about it. Before me was a portrait of an aunt of mine, not particularly close, but someone I once knew well. Her name was Irma D. She had lived in Czechoslovakia and had fallen victim to the war. Exactly where or when she died we still don't know, for she, along

with thousands of others, just disappeared under the Nazi occupation of her homeland. I found out about her sad end in 1945, when communications were restored with Europe. But this was 1959, and I really had not thought of her for many years. So it was with surprise that I found this sign of life, if you will, from a relative. Of course I went to my family album on returning home, to make sure it was she. I did not have the identical picture, but I had a group photograph taken more or less about the same period of her life. In this group shot, Irma is the girl on the right. The one on the left is my late mother, and the one in the middle a mutual school friend of both girls. This was taken when both sisters were still single; the psychic face, however, dates to her early years of marriage, a period one might think she would have considered her best and happiest years.

I took the psychic likeness and presented it to my father, a total skeptic at that time, without telling him anything about it. Instantly he recognized his late sister-in-law. I tested various other relatives of Irma's, and the results were the same. I was so intrigued with all this that I implored Myers to give us another sitting immediately. He acceded to my request and on August 6, 1959, we met again at the Myers' apartment. This time photographic film rather than paper was to be used, and a camera was brought into the room. The camera itself was a bellows type using 120-size film, and there was nothing unusual about its appearance. Myers uses cut film rather than roll film, and the bellows seemed to be in perfect condition when I examined the camera. But there is romance connected with the history of this old camera. It used to belong to the celebrated British psychic photographers William Hope and, later, Mrs. Deane, and passed into Myers' hands in 1930, coming with him to America five years later.

Again present were the photograper Charles Hagedorn and attorney Jacob Gerstein, along with two ladies, Gail Benedict, a publicist, and Mrs. Riccardi, an astrologer and artist. Hagedorn and Gerstein had bought the film at Kodak in New York, and the materials were in Hagedorn's possession until the moment when he and Gerstein loaded the camera in full view of the two ladies and myself. Farther back in the apartment, a group of about ten other persons watched the entire experiment, without taking part in it. It took somewhat longer to develop the exposed film than the paper of the first experiment, but again strange "extras" appeared on the film. In addition, the paper experiment was repeated and several faces appeared on the sheets, none of them, however, known to me or identified. This is not surprising, as psychic photography mediums are rare and the number of persons wishing to communicate from "over there" presumably very great. For what is more vital than to let those left behind know that life does go on? I kept in touch with John Myers after this experiment, but we did not try our hands again at it for the moment.

One day in 1960 I visited his office and he told me of some pictures he had recently taken by himself. I realized that these were not as valid as those taken under my eyes, but it seemed to me rather ludicrous to assume that Myers would spend an evening trying to defraud himself! So I asked to be shown the pictures. Strangely, Myers felt compelled to show me but one of the pictures. I blanched when I looked at it. Though not as sharp as an "ordinary" photograph, the portait was clearly that of a dear friend of mine who had died unhappily and very young not long before. At no time had I discussed her with Myers, nor had Myers ever met her in life. To be doubly sure I showed the picture to the young lady's mother and found her agreeing with me. At various seances and sittings this girl had made her presence known to me, often through strange mediums who didn't even know my name or who had never met me until then. So it did not exactly come as a shock to see this further proof of continued desire to communicate. But it was not until the summer of 1961 that Myers and I again discussed a major experiment. For one thing, he travels a great deal; and for another, I did not wish to subject him to repetitive experiments when his time was valuable. I wanted to try and add new areas of exploration each time.

But when a major television program came to me with the request to put together a "package" of psychic experiments, I decided to include John Myers and his psychic photography prominently. It was not easy to convince him to step into this kind of limelight, with all its limitations and pressures, but in the end he agreed to come. We made our conditions known, and Mike Wallace accepted them on behalf of the show, called *PM East,* produced then by Channel 5, New York. Wallace, a total skeptic, was to purchase ordinary photographic paper in a shop of his own choice and keep it upon his person until air time. This he did, and the sealed, untampered-with paper was produced by him when the three of us went on camera. The developing and fixation liquids as well as the bowls were also supplied by the studio. Myers waited patiently in the wings while other segments of the program were telecast. All this time Wallace had the paper and liquids under his control. Finally we proceeded to take our seats onstage, with Myers on my left and Wallace on my right, perched on wooden stools without backs. The sole source of light now was an overhead yellow bulb, 60 watts in strength, and all the studio lights were turned off.

Immediately upon being on camera, the experiment began. When Wallace opened the package of sealed papers, and threw them one by one into the first liquid, immediately forms started to appear where no forms should appear, as we were dealing with totally virgin photographic paper. If by some freak condition these papers could have been exposed, then they should at the very least have appeared identical. This, however, was not the case;

several were totally blank, while others showed amorphous shapes and figures, one a human arm, one a head and one an as yet indistinct face. At this point a commercial made continuation of the experiment impossible, and the results were less than conclusive as far as the television audience was concerned. Something had of course appeared on the unexposed papers, but what? After the show I examined the dried prints carefully. One of them clearly showed a very fine portait of my late mother, who had died exactly four years before the experiment took place. Now I had not thought of having my late mother put in an appearance, so to speak, to convince the skeptics of survival, nor had John Myers any access to my family album. In fact Myers did not know that my mother had passed away.

Certainly Mike Wallace did not manufacture this picture, for he was and probably still is a firm nonbeliever in the possibility of personal survival. And I, as the researcher, certainly would know better than to produce a fake picture of my own mother if I intended to put over a trick. If anyone's mother, then Wallace's or Myers', certainly not my own, when I was the one person who did have access to a likeness of my mother! The fact that the portrait which thus appeared is that of my late mother is less important than the fact that *any* face appeared at all, for even *that* is paranormal. Even if Myers had wanted to forge this psychic photograph, he would not have been able to do so. The picture of my mother in the family album is not accessible and had to be searched out from storage by me in order to match it up with the psychic image. I also had the negative stored away. The similarity is striking, notably the form of the nose and the parting of the hair; but there is a certain *glow* about the psychic photograph that is not present in the portrait made during her lifetime. The white, cottonlike substance surrounding the face is what I call a "matrix," made up from substance drawn from Myers' body in some fashion and, in my opinion, superimposed upon the light-sensitive paper, thus making it, in addition, *psychically* sensitive. Upon this "film upon a film," then, a thought form of my late mother was imbedded, very much like a wire photo, except that the machine that made this possible was Myers' *body*.

Controlled experiments of this kind have established that communications from the so-called dead can indeed be received under conditions excluding any form of fraud, delusion or self-delusion. Needless, perhaps, to add that no financial rewards whatever were involved for Myers in this experiment.

My next session with John Myers came about as a result of the interest taken by a United Press reporter named Pat Davis in the subject. I requested of John Myers that we try another experiment, and he agreed to do so on April 25, 1964. On this occasion the photographic paper was purchased by a trio of outsiders, namely Dr. S. A. Bell, a dentist, a lady associate of the doctor's, and Miss Lee Perkins of New York City. They accompanied Myers to a store of their own selection, where the paper was bought and initialed by them in the usual manner. Myers of course never touched the package. Three packages had been bought from a batch of photographic paper, presumed to be identical in all respects. The initialed three packages were then placed in a large envelope and the envelope sealed and stapled in the presence of attorney Jacob Gerstein, whose affidavit I have before me. Mr. Gerstein then took charge of the paper and kept it with him until that evening when he brought it along to the Myers apartment for the experiment.

In full view of all those present—about a dozen observers unfamiliar with the subject matter, plus Miss Davis and myself—Gerstein placed the three packages on the table and brought out three basins filled with developing and fixation liquids and water. Pat Davis, who had never met John Myers until then, now stepped forward and, on Myers' suggestion, picked one of the three packages, which again was examined by me and Mr. Gerstein carefully as to possible violations. There were none. The reporter, Miss Davis, then opened the package and, one by one, placed the photographic paper sheets contained in it into the first pan. All this was in full electric light, with the observers standing close by around the table.

As soon as the sheets touched the first liquid, forms and faces began to appear on them, varying from sheet to sheet. Among them was a clear likeness of the late Frank Navroth, immediately identified by Jacob Gerstein, who knew this man before his death. Another photograph turned out to be that of a young girl who had passed on five or six years ago and was identified by one of the observers present, Dan Kriger, an oil executive. Several people recognized the likeness of the late Congressman Adolph Sabath also. Pat Davis then requested that Myers leave the room so that we could determine whether his bodily nearness had any influence on the outcome of the experiment. Myers agreed and went to another part of the apartment. Pat Davis then took the second of the packages and opened it and again submerged the sheets in it exactly as she had done with the first package. Nothing happened. All sheets were blank and exactly alike, a little fogged from the exposure to the strong room light, but without any distinguishing marks whatever. She then opened the third and last package and did the same. Again nothing appeared on the sheets. Finally we used a few sheets still remaining in the first package, and again the results were negative as long as Myers was not at least within the same room.

John Myers is not the only reputable psychic photography medium. For many years I have known and worked with New Yorker Betty Ritter in cases involving her major talents as a clairvoyant. She is a medium who supplies valid information from the so-called dead and

3. Betty Ritter photograph showing ecto-plastic concentrations.

HOW THIS PICTURE WAS OBTAINED.

Time: *1955. Evening.*

Place: *Reverend Boyd's spiritualist church in New York City, during a quasi-public demonstration of Reverend M. Heaney.*

Light conditions: *Normal room light (artificial). No strong reflectors of any kind.*

Camera: *Old-type bellows camera (Kodak), size 116.*

Film: *Kodak, medium-fast film.*

Exposure: *1/25 second.*

Operator: *Betty Ritter.*

Developing and printing: *Local photography shop.*

predicts events before they become objective reality. In this area Betty Ritter is excellent, and I have written of her powers elsewhere. But lately she has also developed her psychic photography to a point where it deserves to be taken very seriously.

Miss Ritter is a middle-aged woman of Italian descent, a pensioner who lives quietly in New York and occasionally sees friends of friends who want a professional "reading" or a psychic consultation. She is a sincere spiritualist and also a devoted Catholic. Any thought of fraud or commercialism is completely alien to her character, and she has remained a person of very modest circumstances. On the occasions when I requested photographic prints of her negatives she would not even ask for her own expenses. That such a person should be subjected to the cheap harassment of sensation-bent radio or television personalities is of course regrettable, and Betty has since learned not to be drawn into that type of activity.

From about 1955 on, Betty has obtained unusual photographs with her old-fashioned bellows camera, results that came as much as a surprise to her as to the people she photographed. She is guided by an intuitive feeling that she should photograph the audiences where psychic energies might be present, perhaps as a result of large-scale production of thought forms, prayers, and other man-made force fields. She has since then taken her camera with her whenever going to a spiritualist church or meeting, or when sitting privately with people whom she knows well enough to be relaxed with. I have often examined her camera and found it in perfect working order. She uses standard film and average developing laboratories; only in the past few months has she finally learned to print from her negatives, atlhough she still does not develop them herself. By no means is Betty Ritter a photographic technician. Some of the many pictures I have in my files that were taken by her, were snapped in my presence, others under conditions I consider satisfactory. I have selected four outstanding photographs from them, although each photograph is merely one of several similar ones obtained on the same roll of film and under similar conditions.

Both the medium and I consider the white lines to the left and the round ball on the right to be concentrations of psychic energy. They cannot be explained by any kind of faulty equipment or materials. Pictures of this type are not too rare, and there seems to be a connection between the number of persons present in the room and the intensity of the phenomena. If ectoplasm is a substance drawn from the bodies of emotionally stimulated sitters, and I think it is, then this substance must assemble in some form or shape before it can be utilized via thought direction to perform some intelligent task. I suggest that these streaks, known as "rods," are the raw materials that are used also in materializations of the dead, when these are genuine phenomena, and in poltergeist cases, when objects seemingly move of their own volition. This material, isolated some years ago in London and found to be a moist, smelly whitish substance related to albumen, undoubtedly comes from the body glands of the medium and her sitters or helpers. It is later returned to the sources, or that portion of it not used up at the end of the seance. It can be molded like wax into any form or shape. Strange as this may sound, it is thought direction that does the molding.

In the case of the spiritualist seance picture no such molding has taken place, and what we see on the picture is merely the free ectoplasm as it is manufactured and assembled. The naked eye does not normally see this, of course. But then the human eye does not register much of the spectrum, either. The combination of sensitive camera and sensitive photographer or operator seems to be the catalyst to put this material onto photographic film. Just how this works we don't know fully as yet, but it happens frequently under similar conditions and in all such cases faulty materials or cameras have been ruled out.

In the second picture we see how the ectoplasm can be used to bring home a definite message or thought form.

One of those present at this small gathering in Reverend Boyd's church was Helen M., whose father had died seven years before. He had lost a leg in his physical life. The communicator, through the medium, wanted to prove his identity in some form and proposed to show his severed leg as a kind of signature, while at the same time making a point of his having two good legs once more in *his* world.

On the print (which matches the negative which I have seen) the white substance of the "new" leg is superimposed on the leg of the sitter. It is to be noted also that there appear to be two extra hands in the picture, while the rest of the photograph is sharp, pointing to supernormal origin of the extras rather than conventional double exposure—the rest of the picture is sharply defined. It is my opinion that ectoplasm was molded via thought into the desired shapes and the latter then made capable of being photographed.

On May 10, 1963, Betty Ritter visited my home for a private sitting, during which she felt herself moved to take our picture with her bellows camera. At the time my wife was expecting our little girl fairly soon, and Betty Ritter assured us that my late mother was particularly concerned over her and me and was "present" during the sitting.

It is rather remarkable that my picture is almost totally wiped out and covered by some form of ectoplastic curtain, with an extra pair of arms clearly visible above mine. I, of course, never budged during the taking of this picture, a fact that can also be ascertained by the lack of double exposure in the sharp picture

4. One-legged communicator showing ecto-plastic leg superimposed on medium as means of identification in this Betty Ritter photograph.

HOW THIS PICTURE WAS OBTAINED.

Time: *February 11, 1963.*

Place: *Reverend Boyd's spiritualist church in New York City.*

Light conditions: *Normal room light.*

Camera: *Kodak roll film camera, bellows, size 116.*

Film: *Medium-fast black-and-white Kodak 116.*

Exposure: *1/25 second.*

Operator: *Betty Ritter.*

Developing and printing: *Local photography shop.*

5. Holzer partially obscured and mother's hands visible beside his own in this Betty Ritter picture taken at Holzer's house.

HOW THIS PICTURE WAS OBTAINED.

Time:	*May 10, 1963.*
Place:	*My home, New York City.*
Light conditions:	*Normal electric room light.*
Camera:	*Kodak size 116 bellows camera*
Film:	*Medium-fast black-and-white Kodak film 116.*
Exposure:	*About half a second from firm surface (piano).*
Operator:	*Betty Ritter.*
Developing and printing:	*Local photography shop.*

of my wife and of the lamp and plant behind her. The superimposed fingers of the right hand above my own right hand are rather different from mine; they are, in fact, thinner and bonier than my own fingers, and it so happens that that is exactly what my late mother's hands and fingers looked like.

As the psychic photographer develops his or her skill, the extras become more sophisticated until they eventually are faces or entire figures. With Betty Ritter it started with concentrations of power or ectoplasm, and later included such higher forms of imagery as hands, a cross symbol and, eventually, writing. The last came about in the following manner: In 1965 I had recommended a young lady named Trudy S. to Betty. I myself had unsuccessfully tried to break the hold a dead person evidently had on her. This was probably due to the fact that Trudy herself is psychic and therefore supplies the desired entrance way. The attentions of this young man, who died in a car accident and had been a friend of the young girl's during his lifetime, were not welcomed by Miss S. after his death. I thought that perhaps Betty Ritter, being a strong medium (which I decidedly am not), might be able to "outdraw" the unwelcome intruder and, as it turned out, I was right in my suggestion. Betty managed to help Miss S. a great deal, which was the more welcome, as I had found the girl well balanced in every respect and leading a normal and interesting life. Involvement with the occult was the last thing she desired.

6. *"ROME" in ectoplastic 'cloud' in upper left on psychic photo taken by Betty Ritter with sitter Trudy S. in 1965.*

HOW THIS PICTURE WAS OBTAINED.

Time:	*March 3, 1965.*
Place:	*Betty Ritter's apartment, New York.*
Light conditions:	*Ordinary room light.*
Camera:	*Old-style Kodak bellows camera, size 116.*
Film:	*Medium-fast black-and-white Kodak 116.*
Exposure:	*1/25 second.*
Operator:	*Betty Ritter.*
Developing and printing:	*Local photography shop.*

During the time when Trudy S. went to see Betty Ritter to break the hold of the dead man, she also, quite naturally, had a boy friend in her physical world. But the intruder from beyond the veil kept interfering until the couple broke up, largely because of the situation. On March 3, 1965, Trudy S. had a sitting with Betty during which Betty took some photographs. On one of them, imbedded in the well-known "cotton wool" of psychic photography, there appears the word ROME in black letters. Nothing in the negative, the camera, the film or the paper can account for this writing. Why ROME? At the time of this sitting Trudy's boy friend was in Italy and on his way to Rome. Was Betty's camera catching a thought form from Trudy's unconscious mind, or was she recording a key word concerning Trudy's future relationship with this man? In either case it was an unusual example of psychic photography and certainly paranormal in the accepted sense of this term.

Dr. Andrew von Salza, a West Coast physician originally without any interest in psychic matters, began to realize that he had a strange gift for psychic photography. He is a jolly and successful man in his fifties and holds medical degrees from the Universities of Berlin and Tartu (Estonia). A leading rejuvenation specialist in California, he was nothing more than an amateur shutterbug without the slightest interest in anything supernormal or psychic.

Unexpected and totally unwarranted "extras" have appeared on his photographs, both those taken with regular cameras and with the speedy Polaroid type. He had known of my interest in psychic research through a mutual friend, Gail Benedict, the public-relations director of the Savoy-Hilton, where he usually stayed. Although I had heard about his strange encounters with this subject, my only previous meeting with the doctor was on a social occasion a year before, where others were present and when the chance to discuss the matter deeply did not present itself. At that time, too, Dr. von Salza met my wife, Catherine, and was told that she was of Russian descent, to which he remarked that he was a Balt himself. But neither the doctor nor my wife went into any detailed history of her background.

Finally, in the second week of March, 1966, von Salza arrived in New York on business and unexpectedly telephoned me, offering to experiment in my presence, as I had so long desired him to do. We arranged for a get-together at our house on Sunday, March 13, and I asked Gail Benedict to bring the doctor over. In addition, a friend of Miss Benedict's, Mrs. Marsha Slansky, a designer and not particularly experienced in matters of psychic research, joined us as an additional observer. Shortly after the arrival of the guests, the doctor suddenly requested that my wife seat herself in an armchair at the far end of the living room, because he felt the urge to take a picture of her. It was at this point that I examined the camera and film and satisfied myself that no fraud could have taken place.

The first picture taken showed a clear super-imposition, next to my wife, of a female figure, made up of a white, semitransparent substance. As a trained historian I immediately recognized this as an attempted portrait of Catherine the Great. The sash of her order, which she liked to wear in many of her official portraits, stood out quite clearly on this print. We continued to expose the rest of the pack, and still another pack which I purchased at a corner drugstore a little later that evening, but the results were negative except for some strange light streaks which could not be accounted for normally. The doctor handed me the original picture, and the following day I had a laboratory try to make me a duplicate which I was to send him for the record. Unfortunately the results were poor, the sash did not show at all in the repro-duction, and I was told that this was the best they could do because the original was a Polaroid picture and not as easily copied as an ordinary print. At any rate I mailed this poor copy to Andrew von Salza in San Francisco with my explanation and regrets. To my sur-prise we received a letter from him, dated March 25, 1966, in which he enclosed two pictures of the same subject. Only this time the figure of Catherine the Great was sharp and detailed, much more so than in the original pic-ture and, in fact, superimposed upon the whit-ish outline of the first photograph. The whole thing looked so patently fraudulent at first glance that I requested exact data on how this second "round" was taken. Not that I suspected

the doctor of malpractice, but I am a researcher and cannot afford to be noble.

Von Salza obliged. When he had received my poor copy of his fine psychic picture, he had tacked it to a blank wall in a corner of his San Francisco apartment in order to rephotograph it. Why he did this he cannot explain, except that he felt "an urge" to do so. I have his signed statement to the effect that he used a Crown Graphic camera with Polaroid back, size 4 x 5, an enlarging lens, opening of F/32, with the camera mounted on a tripod about a yard or less away from the subject. His ex-posure for the rephotographing experiment was one second by daylight plus one 150-watt lamp.

Furthermore, Dr. von Salza offered to repeat the experiment in my presence whenever I came to San Francisco. What struck me as remarkable about the whole business was of course the fact, unknown to the doctor, that my wife Catherine is a direct sixth-generation descendant of Catherine the Great. This was not discussed with him until after the first picture was obtained. Nevertheless Gail Bene-dict reports that on the way over to our apart-ment, von Salza suddenly and cryptically asked, "Why do I keep thinking of Catherine the Great?" Now had he wanted to defraud us, surely he would not have tipped his hand in this manner. The two rephotographed pictures sent to me by the doctor are not identical; on one of them a crown appears over my wife's head! I should like to mention here also that several psychics with whom my wife and I have "sat,"

7. a. Contemporary print of Catherine the Great showing similar sash of order; note also outstretched arm, contour of hairdo.

b. Dr. Andrew von Salza took this remarkable picture of Catherine Holzer in her home; white extra of Mrs. Holzer's direct ancestor Catherine of Russia on right.

HOW THIS PICTURE WAS OBTAINED.

Time:	*March 13, 1966, 9 P.M.*
Place:	*The living room of Hans and Catherine Holzer's apartment, New York City.*
Light conditions:	*Ordinary room lights, all shielded from reflection and glare, occasional lamps, but no overhead ceiling lights.*
Camera:	*Polaroid 103, the "better" model of the line.*
Film:	*Polaroid film pack, obtained from photographic dealer and examined by me prior to insertion in camera, and found untouched.*
Exposure:	*1/100 second.*
Operator:	*Dr. Andrew von Salza of San Francisco, California.*

b.

8. *a. Second impression of Catherine shows it similar to contemporary prints. This picture was produced under Holzer's control.*

b. Note outstretched arm of Catherine holding crown. Taken in presence of investigator.

8. *a.*

b.

who knew nothing whatever about my wife or her background, have remarked that they "saw" a royal personality protecting my wife. New York medium Betty Ritter even described her by name as Catherine. It is true also that my wife has for years had a strong interest in the historical Catherine, and finds herself drawn frequently to books dealing with the life of the Empress. Although her sisters and brothers are equally close in descent to the Russian ruler, they do not show any particular affinity toward her.

The whole matter of these pictures was so outlandish that I felt either they were clever frauds and that I was being duped (although I did not see how this was possible under my stringent conditions) or that the material had to be factual, appearances to the contrary. Circumstantial evidence can be very misleading in so controversial a subject as psychic photography and I was determined not to allow opinions, pro or con, to influence my findings in this case.

Consequently, I went to San Francisco in the middle of May, 1966, to test the good doctor. In my presence he took the original picture and mounted it on the wall, then placed film into his Crown Graphic camera with a Polaroid back. I inspected camera and film and nothing had been tampered with. The first two pictures yielded results; again a clear imprint of Catherine the Great was superimposed upon the whitish outline of the original. But this time Catherine extended an arm toward her

descendant! In her extended right hand the Empress tendered a crown to my wife, but the two pictures are otherwise somewhat different in detail and intensity, although taken one after the other under identical light and exposure conditions *in my presence*. At this point I confess I became somewhat impatient and said aloud, "I wish Catherine would give us a message. What is she trying to tell us?" As if I had committed *lèse majesté*, the psychic camera fell silent; the next picture showed nothing further than the whitish outline. We discontinued the experiment at this point. I inspected the camera once more and then left the doctor.

Before we parted I once more inspected the camera. It looked just like any ordinary Crown Graphic does, except for the Polaroid back, but even that is now being used by better photographers everywhere. The enlarging lens was still set at F/32; the exposure, I knew, had been just one second, using ordinary daylight reinforced by one 150-watt lamp. Dr. von Salza later sent me a cheerful note in which he said, "Seeing is believing, but even seeing, so many cannot believe, including myself." He found the whole situation very amusing and made no serious effort to do much about it scientifically, except that he did cooperate with me whenever I asked him to.

His first encounter with the uncanny was in 1963, when the widow of a colleague of his, Dr. Benjamin Sweetland, asked him to do a photo portrait of her. Von Salza obliged, but imagine their surprise when the face of the late husband appeared superimposed on a lamp-shade in the room. No double exposure, no fraud, no rational explanation for this phenomenon could be found, although von Salza, with his worldly training, insisted that "there had to be some other explanation!" To test this situation, he decided to photograph the widow Sweetland again, but with another camera and outdoors. Using a Leica and color film, and making sure that all was in order, he found to his amazement that one of the twenty exposures showed the late doctor's face against the sky.

Dismissing the whole incident for want of an explanation and trying his best to forget it, he was again surprised when another incident took place. This time he was merely using up the last picture in his roll, shooting at random against the wall of his own room. When the roll was developed, there appeared on the wall the face of a young girl that had not been there when he took the picture. He was upset by this and found himself discussing the matter with a friend and patient of his by the name of Mrs. Pierson. She asked to be shown the picture. On inspection, she blanched. Andrew von Salza had somehow photographed the face of her "dead" young daughter. Although the doctor knew of the girl's untimely death, he had never seen her in life.

Several more incidents of this nature convinced the doctor that he had somehow stumbled onto a very special talent, like it or not. He began to investigate the subject to find out if others also had his kind of "problems." Among the people interested in psychic phenomena in the San Francisco area was a lady by the name of Evelyn Nielsen, with whom von Salza later shared a number of experiments. He soon discovered that her presence increased the incidence rate of psychic "extras" on his exposures, although Miss Nielsen herself never took a psychic photograph without Andrew von Salza's presence, proving that it was he who was the mainspring of the phenomena.

In early May of 1965 I went to San Francisco to observe the doctor at work—psychic photography work, that is, not his regular occupation, which is never open to anyone but the subjects! I fortified myself with the company of two "outsiders," my sister-in-law, Countess Marie Rose Buxhoeveden, and a friend, social worker Lori Wynn, who came with me to von Salza's apartment. There we met the doctor, Evelyn Nielsen and Mrs. Sweetland, as well as two other ladies, friends of the doctor's, who had been sympathetic to the subject at hand. It was late afternoon, and we all had dinner engagements, so we decided to get started right away.

With a sweeping gesture the doctor invited me to inspect the camera, already on its tripod facing the wall, or, as he called it, his "ghost corner," for he had always had best results by shooting away from the bright windows toward the darker portion of his big living room. The walls were bare except for an Indian

9. During San Francisco experiment with Dr. Andrew von Salza, several portrait "extras" appeared on Polaroid film. Others on couch are Evelyn Nielsen, associate and Dr. von Salza and friends.

HOW PICTURES 9–11 WERE OBTAINED.

Time: May, 1965, late afternoon, bright sun.

Place: Apartment of Dr. Andrew von Salza, San Francisco, California.

Light conditions: Daylight coming into the room.

Camera: Crown Graphic with Polaroid film back, 4 x 5.

Film: Polaroid black-and-white film, fast.

Exposure: F/16, 1/250 second.

Operator: Dr. Andrew von Salza.

Developing: Instantaneous by von Salza in full view of witnesses.

Witnesses: Evelyn Nielsen, Marie Rose Buxhoeveden, Lori Wynn, Mrs. Sweetland, two other ladies, and I.

10. *a. Partially completed exposure of Polaroid film appears to be writing on wall; operator von Salza seated on right. Camera was tripped automatically.*

b. Next exposure clarifies smoky writing as the word "WAR" with late President Kennedy's portrait above it. Also taken under Hans Holzer's complete control and supervision.

*11. Psychic photo taken in Holzer's presence
    by Dr. von Salza shows portrait of the
    elder Rockefeller in center.*

wall decoration and a portrait of the doctor. In a way, they reminded me of motion-picture screens in their smoothness and blue-gray texture. But there was absolutely nothing on those walls that could be blamed for what eventually appeared "on" them.

I stepped up to the camera and looked inside, satisfying myself that nothing had been pasted in the bellows or gizmo, or on the lens. Then I looked at the film, which was an ordinary Polaroid film pack, black-and-white, and there was no evidence of its having been tampered with. The only way to do this, by the way, would have been to slit open the pack and insert extraneous matter into the individual pieces of film, something requiring great skill, total darkness and time. Even then traces of the cuttings would have to appear. The pack Dr. von Salza used was fresh and untouched.

The room was bright enough, as light streamed in from the windows opposite the L-shaped couch which lined the walls. The seven of us now sat down on this couch. Von Salza set the camera and exposed the first piece of film. Within sight of all of us, he developed the film in the usual fast Polaroid manner and then showed it to me. Over our heads there appear clearly four extra portraits, and the wall can be seen through them. I myself did not recognize any of the four in this instance. The doctor continued, this time including himself in the picture by presetting the camera and then taking his place next to Evelyn Nielsen on the couch.

The second picture, when developed, evoked some gasps of recognition from the audience. Four faces of various size appeared and a light-shaft (of psychic energy?) also was now evident on the left side of the photograph. But the gasp of recognition was due to the likeness of the late John D. Rockefeller, Sr. I might add here that this gentleman must have an avid interest in communicating with the world he left at age ninety some years ago. His face has appeared in other instances of psychic photography, especially in Britain with John Myers.

Again von Salza cocked the shutter and prepared for an exposure. This time the results were puzzling, for all that showed were some smoky outlines, possibly an attempt at writing letters. I asked that another picture be taken immediately to see if we could improve on this. We could, and the result was picture number four. This time the letters clearly spell the word WAR, and above the letter A appears a portrait of the late John F. Kennedy. Immediately, speculation arose whether the late President wanted to warn us of impending war or lament the present conflict. My first reaction on seeing the Kennedy image was one of doubt and worry. It had to be faked. But how? I went over every detail of the experiment again and, after the meeting was over, inspected the camera, the film, the room once more.

Certainly this picture could have been faked or imitated by a clever man, but *not* under the circumstances under which it was obtained in my presence. This is the whole point: not the question of whether a psychic photo *could* be forged but whether in fact it was or wasn't under the watchful eyes of the experienced observer. And, unless a miracle even greater than that of genuine psychic photography took place, of which none of us are as yet aware, this Kennedy photo was not a forgery or the result of willful manipulation of any kind.

It should be kept in mind, in this connection, that Dr. von Salza never showed the pictures publicly, never made any claims whatever about them, and that he himself is as puzzled about them as any outsider might be. This curiosity made him continue the experiments privately usually with Evelyn Nielsen his only associate. In the same manner as in my presence, they obtained a number of interesting photographs, which I am also showing here. For while it is true that I was not physically in the room when they were taken, they were produced under identical circumstances and with identical materials and tools as those that were taken earlier in my presence.

I am satisfied that they are not fraudulent because of the total absence of a motive, because similar pictures obtained by the same methods in my presence were definitely genuine and because of my close relationship with, and knowledge of, the two people involved.

The first of these four pictures is more likely to bring forth doubts than any other photograph of this kind. This is because of the cut-out quality of Lincoln's portrait in the upper right corner next to Kennedy's. Now this fact is not exactly new; all psychic photographers have at one time or other been accused of fraud because of *appearances*. The majority of—but not all—psychic "extras" (portraits) are not "new" faces of the dead but faithful reproductions of photographs or paintings of them while in the flesh. This is so universally true that one would have to condemn almost all psychic photos taken over the past hundred years, including some highly evidential tests, if one were to consider the reproduction of "cut-out"-type photographs as fraudulent *per se*. The obvious is not necessarily true, as circumstantial evidence tends to be misleading at times.

Communicators have frequently explained the need for a discarnate person to visualize *first* a photograph of himself before being able to transmit a thought image of that portrait to the medium and thence to photographic paper or film. Certainly, one can cut out a photograph and paste it up on another and rephotograph the whole thing with results not so different from what we have here. The point again is that it does not necessarily *follow*. Bear in mind that the conditions under which psychic extras are obtained are the most important part of the evidence.

The next picture is extraordinary for the large number of extras it contains. Among the many unknown (to me) faces, there appear to be that of Lee Harvey Oswald, and that of Marilyn Monroe, his in the center and hers toward the bottom left. The typed inscription across her portrait reads MISTAKE—NOT SUICIDE. Several psychics have reported similar messages from the "dead" actress since her passing. It is noteworthy also that a lot of the people thus appearing on psychic photographs are either earthbound persons, those with unfinished business, or persons who are not able to adjust to their state of being in what Dr. Joseph Rhine has called "the world of the mind."

The third picture shows Evelyn Nielsen and two unidentified friends under a strange birdlike extra. This Miss Nielsen explained as being her Indian guide or control. Miss Nielsen is a nonprofessional spiritualist medium. The cottonlike substance, so prominent with this type of phenomenon, is again present below the Indian's portrait.

The fourth picture is remarkable not for its extras—it shows none—but for what happens to the photographer, Dr. von Salza himself. Taken through remote control, the camera shows the good doctor practically dissolved. In my opinion, ectoplasm was forming in the areas around him, but somehow the process was not completed and no faces appeared imbedded in the mass thus produced. Thus the strange picture of a disappearing man. I am looking forward to additional tests and experiments with Andrew von Salza, for as a scien-

tist I am never entirely satisfied until I know all the workings of seeming "miracles" or other wondrous events. In a statement given to me on October 1, 1967, Dr. von Salza concludes, "I have no opinion to offer on these pictures, as I leave the explanations to you. But I do know that they are genuine and constitute an amazing new scientific phenomenon."

Although Sybil Leek, the British author who works with me as a trance medium and psychic, has done extraordinary things in my presence, notably fine trance work and clairvoyance, she has never considered herself a photographic medium. On one or two occasions, many years ago, strange objects did appear on photographs taken of her or in her presence, but she had never pursued the matter.

On a Friday morning in July, 1967, Sybil telephoned me in great agitation. She had just had a very vivid dream, or at any rate fallen into a state similar to the dream state. Someone named Vivien had communicated with her and remarked that she was now going on a holiday. Did I know any Vivien? Why me, I asked. Because this communicator wanted Sybil to call me and tell me. Was there anything more? No, just that much. I pondered the matter. The only Vivien I ever knew personally was a young girl not likely to be on the Other Side as yet. But of course one never knows. I was still pondering the matter when the Saturday newspaper headlines proclaimed the death of Vivien Leigh. It appeared that she had just been dis-

12. Evelyn Nielsen is sitter to Dr. von Salza's camera, with Kennedy and Lincoln appearing as extras. Despite cut-out quality of portraits, Holzer considers this genuine psychic picture as cut-out quality necessary for production of this type picture.

HOW PICTURES 12–15 WERE OBTAINED.

Time:	*1966.*
Place:	*Dr. Andrew von Salza's San Francisco apartment.*
Light conditions:	*Daytime, natural light only.*
Camera:	*Crown Graphic with Polaroid back, 4 x 5.*
Film:	*Polaroid fast film, black-and-white.*
Exposure:	*F/16 and 1/250 second.*
Operator:	*Dr. Andrew von Salza.*
Developing:	*On the spot, by the doctor.*

13. *Abundance of psychic extras in this von Salza photograph includes presumably post-mortem portraits of Marilyn Monroe (with "Mistake—Not Suicide" written across her front) and Lee Harvey Oswald. Sitter Nielsen is seen in right lower corner.*

14. *Indian "guide" of medium Nielsen mani-*
    fests on this Polaroid picture taken by Dr.
    von Salza.

15. *Automatically tripped camera shows von Salza practically invisible as ectoplastic material is building up for "extras" that never made it.*

covered dead in her London apartment, but death might have come to her any time before Saturday, most likely on Friday. Suddenly I saw the connection and called Sybil. Did she know Vivien Leigh at all? She did indeed, although she had not seen her for some time. Years ago Vivien Leigh would consult Sybil in personal matters, for Sybil is pretty good at sorting things out for her friends.

There was definitely a relationship. Nobody in the world knew that Vivien Leigh had died *on Friday*. The discovery was made on Saturday. And yet Sybil had her communication during Thursday night. The date? June 30, 1967. I felt it was the actress' way of saying goodbye and at the same time letting the world know that life continued. That was on Saturday. On Monday Sybil had a visitor at the Stewart Studios, where she is usually staying when in New York. Her visitor, Edmond Hanrahan, was so impressed with the unusual decor of the studio that he decided to take some color pictures with his camera, which he happened to have with him at the time. The date was July 3, 1967. Several pictures were of Sybil Leek. There was nothing remarkable about any of them, except one. Partially obstructing Sybil is the face of a dark-haired woman with an unmistakable profile—that of Vivien Leigh!

Both Sybil and the photographer remember clearly that there was nobody else with them at the time, nor was there anything wrong with either film or camera. The psychic extra seems soft and out of focus, as if the figure had stepped between camera and Sybil, but too close to be fully in focus.

I questioned Mr. Hanrahan about the incident. He admitted that this was not the first time something or someone other than the person he was photographing showed up on a negative. On one particularly chilling occasion he'd been photographing the widow of a man who had been murdered. On the negative the murdered man appeared next to his widow! Mr. Hanrahan lists his occupation as yachtsman; clearly he is not too worried about income, although he does do commercial photography now and then when the spirit moves him.

He owns a yacht named *Parthenia* and lives on it most of the time. An American, about thirty years old, he is somewhat of a mystery man. But there is no mystery about the method he used when the present photograph resulted. Using a Honeywell Pentax 35mm camera and Ektachrome film, he did not employ a flashgun but used all the available room light. He was relieved to hear that there was nothing wrong with his ability as a photographer or his camera, and he could not very well be held accountable for unseen models.

Evelyn England is a professional photographer who has at one time or other worked for most of the big movie studios in Hollywood, where she now lives. Presently, and for some time past, she operates her own photography studio as a commercial photographer. Ever since she was young she had ESP experiences, especially of the gift of finding lost objects under strange circumstances, as if driven by some inner voice. But despite these leanings she had no particular interest in the subject itself and merely took it for granted that others also had ESP, and that was that.

One of her jobs is photographing high-school graduations. So it was merely a routine assignment when she was called upon to take the picture of a certain mathematics teacher we will call Mr. G. The date was Saturday, April 3, 1965. He was the last one of the faculty to come in for his portrait. Sunday her studio was closed. On Monday she developed and re-touched the print, and Tuesday morning she mailed it to the school. A few hours later she received a phone call from the school principal. Had Mr. G. come in yet for his sitting? Yes, Miss England answered, and informed the principal that the print was already in the mail. At this there was a slight pause. Then the principal informed her that Mr. G. had died unexpectedly on Sunday.

In May of the same year a man came into her studio who remarked that he felt she had a good deal of ESP, being himself interested in such matters. Miss England took his portrait. He then came in to pick his choice from the proofs. She then placed the print into the developer, but to her amazement, it was not Mr. H.'s face that came up! It was Mr. G.'s, the dead mathematics teacher's, face. A moment

16. British psychic Sybil Leek partially eclipsed by psychic photograph of erstwhile friend Vivian Leigh. Picture was taken about a week after star's death by semi-professional photographer-yachtsman Edmond Hanrahan.

HOW THIS PICTURE WAS OBTAINED.

Time: *July 3, 1967. Afternoon.*

Place: *Stewart Studios, New York.*

Light conditions: *Room light, electric. No flash.*

Camera: *Honeywell Pentax, 35mm.*

Film: *Ektachrome, artificial light (20 exposures).*

Exposure: *1/50 second, open lens.*

Operator: *Edmond Hanrahan.*

Developing and printing: *Local photography shop (via Kodak).*

later, while she was still staring in disbelief, the portrait of her client Mr. H. came up on the same print, stronger than the first portrait and facing the opposite way from it.

Miss England is a very meticulous photographer. It is her habit never to leave an undeveloped print around. She will always develop each print fully when she does it, never leaving half-finished prints behind. No one but she uses the studio. There just wasn't any "rational" explanation for what had happened. The smiling face of the late mathematics teacher was there to remind her that life was not over for him—or perhaps a token of gratitude for having been the last person to have seen him "alive." Hastily, Miss England printed another picture of Mr. H., and it was just a normal photograph.

Since then other "dead" persons have used her skills to manifest themselves, but this incident has been the most remarkable one in her psychic life.

17. *Professional commercial photographer Evelyn England accidentally produced psychic photo of dead client while developing another man's portrait.*

HOW THIS PICTURE WAS OBTAINED.

Time: *May, 1965.*

Place: *Evelyn England's photography studio, Los Angeles.*

Light conditions: *Studio printing lights.*

Camera: *A standard printer.*

Paper: *Standard printing paper.*

Operator: *Evelyn England, professional commercial photographer.*

The Electrified Woman: Experiments with Florence

Whenever Florence Sternfels referred to her unusual powers she called them simply "the forces." Not one to be very specific in scientific matters, the late psychometrist (a person who can touch an object belonging to someone and thereby learn facts about that person) from Edgewater, New Jersey, was in great awe of her own supernormal abilities and left the explanations to others. Not that she wasn't proud of her achievements. She did help the FBI on several occasions, and was a whiz at finding missing persons. She was not merely a very good "reader," a clairvoyant, but a lot more than that. Her body definitely had strange qualities. For one thing, she was able to put the telephone or the electric system in her house out of commission by merely touching it. In the end she had to be very careful about this strange quirk of hers, because the telephone company saw nothing humorous in having to come time and again to fix the apparatus. So Florence had always someone—usually her brother, Nelson—to take care of mundane matters for her, while she did the psychic work.

My acquaintanceship with Florence goes back many years. I met her through a study group interested in ESP research and finally accepted her invitation to come out to her house and try her for mediumship. For Florence was never satisfied to be a really fine psychometrist—she wanted to develop deep trance as well. On one particular occasion in 1952 I went to New Jersey armed not only with a high-speed camera and fast black-and-white film, but also a highly treasured wooden box. This box, given to us by a physician friend, contained a piece of medical X-ray film, properly shielded from any and all light or other radiation. Thus we could use it with confidence, secure in the knowledge that if anything appeared on the film at all it would not be due to light leaks or other faults of the equipment.

I placed this wooden box containing the film underneath Florence's foot. On her forehead and arms I fastened several small pieces of infrared film encased in heavy black paper. After Florence had gone into a kind of trance we turned on the lights, which had been extinguished, and took off the film. The film, including the big box with the X-ray film, was then sent to a lab for developing. Imagine my surprise when I saw what had shown up on the X-ray negative. She had exposed this film with her foot—certainly a first in photography, psychic or normal. Was this a crude impression of her own self, seated as she was in her wooden chair? Was it someone else's figure? Surely nothing should have shown up on the negative, for it had never been exposed to either light or radiation of any known kind. Or had it? Had not Florence's own body been the source of radiation, allowing her to be a kind of human camera?

Several months after this initial experiment I returned to Florence's house. In the meantime, her son had died and what had appeared

18. Medical X-ray picture taken with Florence Sternfels' foot, shows figure in chair. No camera was used.

HOW THIS PICTURE WAS OBTAINED.

Time: 1952.

Place: Florence Sternfels' residence, Edgewater, New Jersey.

Light conditions: Total darkness.

Camera: No camera.

Film: Medical X-ray in heavy wooden box.

Exposure: About an hour.

Operator: Florence Sternfels.

Developing: Medical lab in area.

Printing: United Camera shops, New York.

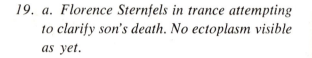

19. a.

19. *a. Florence Sternfels in trance attempting to clarify son's death. No ectoplasm visible as yet.*

b. Ectoplasm starts forming in solar plexus area.

c. Fully formed ectoplasm shows small dog's head with one ear only formed. Pictures taken with infrared flash.

HOW THESE PICTURES WERE OBTAINED.

Time: 1952.

Place: *Florence Sternfels' residence, Edgewater, New Jersey.*

Light conditions: *Total darkness, black flash-bulbs.*

Camera: *Leica, 35mm.*

Film: *Infrared film. Fresh stock.*

Exposure: *Synchronized flash exposure, about 1/25 to 1/50 second.*

Operator: *Ben Paratore.*

Developing and printing: *Local photography shop.*

b.

c.

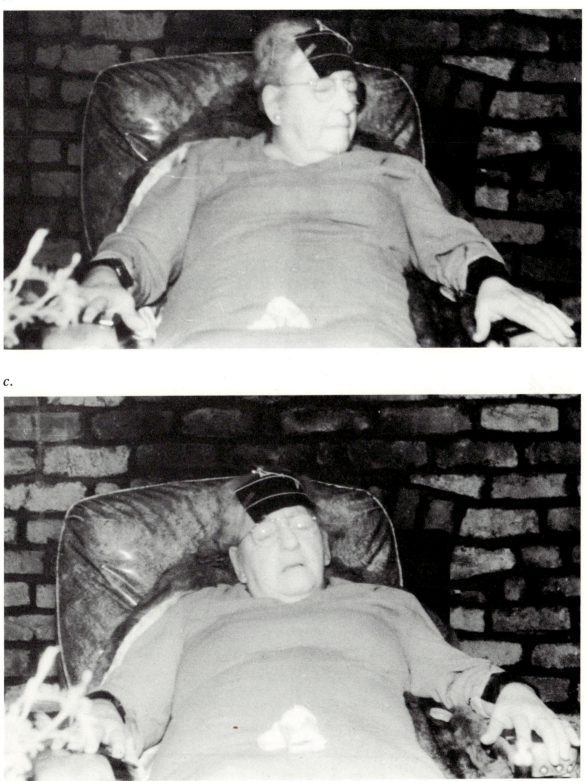

to be a suicide due to asphyxiation in a gas stove, was now open to question. The anguished mother, quite naturally, could not accept the suicide verdict. But there were others in the community who also expressed doubts about the whole matter. The boy had been involved in strange business dealings with men not of the highest caliber, and the possibility of foul play was not entirely impossible. Still, there was no proof, so the case was not being reopened, much as Florence wanted it.

This time I came in the company of two friends, Mr. and Mrs. Ben Paratore. Mr. Paratore brought a 35mm Leica and infrared film, and I brought some black bulbs to be used in conjunction with the experiment. Mr. Paratore, who is an aircraft manufacturing executive, was a skeptic, though willing to observe. We put out the lights and almost total darkness enveloped the medium, who was seated across the room from us, with a table between us on which freshly cut flowers had been placed. The reason for the flowers was not politeness or a sense of romance, but it is one of the beliefs of spiritualists that freshly cut flowers exude a life force that can be used to manufacture ectoplasm, so necessary in psychic photography.

Again, we tied some shielded infrared film to Florence's forehead and arms, while Mr. Paratore got his camera and flashgun ready. As soon as Florence was apparently in deep trance, I asked him to take pictures at regular intervals. I had also brought a metal trumpet with me which I had made myself the previous day. This trumpet, made of completely smooth, virgin aluminum, I then placed next to the medium. After an hour of deep trance, during which mumbling by the medium was the only discernible noise, we gently woke her and turned the lights on again. Immediately I took up the trumpet and found it hot. Now the trumpet had been far enough from Florence to exclude any possibility of her touching it without getting out of her chair, and she did not move, for I was close enough to her to observe her every movement.

In addition to being inexplicably hot, the metal was now covered by several dozen crudely drawn pictures of sorts, one of which seemed to show a man with his head in an oven, and a small dog near him trying to pull him out. Now it so happens that that is precisely what had taken place when Mrs. Sternfels' son had died. His small cocker spaniel had found the master with his head in the oven, and tried to pull him out but, being unable to do so, had died with him, and was so found. The metal trumpet was requested by Florence at the time, and I could not very well refuse the distraught mother what was to her the only sign of life from her late boy. I have never been able to get it back, and Florence herself passed away not long ago.

When the pictures taken by Mr. Paratore in my presence were developed, we discovered to our surprise that a materialization had taken place on Florence's lap. Rising from what is generally called the solar plexus, or the stomach regions where the seat of ectoplasm is said to be, we found at first a white substance forming. Gradually it took on shape and eventually wound up in the form of a small dog's head, with only one ear formed. Noteworthy, too, is the connecting "rod" or link between the flowers and Florence's body. Needless to add that Florence had nothing resting on her lap, nor was there any white object on the table before her that could have been mistaken for the ectoplasm.

Can You Photograph a Ghost?

I think ever since ghosts were talked about in modern times the skeptics must have commented, "Yes, but try and photograph one! Seeing is believing. Anything I can touch, see, hear or smell I'll believe." It would be convenient to agree with this pat philosophy, were it not so patently inadequate. You don't touch, see, hear or smell radio waves, for instance, and yet they are very real and their results can be measured and observed. Mental activity can never be proven objectively to an outsider, as it goes on within the closed confines of man's head. But the consequences of this activity can be observed. Nobody disbelieves thoughts. And yet, sometimes a different yardstick is being used to deal with psychic phenomena. The medium psychically observing an apparition and reporting it in minute detail to the non-psychics concerned with it is exactly as factual as the skeptic having a thought of any kind. Only the environment of our basically materialistic age has taught the skeptic to arbitrarily reject certain mental impressions because they do not conform to the image of the world he has been brought up in. The will to disbelieve regardless of evidence, so long as the evidence is contrary to *accepted* belief, is the strongest and most widespread of all human motivations, even stronger than the will to *believe*.

Despite my firm conviction that ghosts were indeed real in the same sense as radio waves are real and tangible, being made up of electric impulses put together in unique forms called human personalities, I looked for a way to prove this conviction to the outside world. Evidence excluding information obtained by my mediums by ordinary means was piling up, and my books are full of the details. But the Chinese proverb reminds us that one picture is worth more than ten thousand words.

There is a basic difference between a psychic photograph which tends to implement communication between two states of being and is usually the result of experimental desire on the part of a group of people to get results, and the entirely spontaneous, unexpected, unintended photograph of a ghost in his haunted habitat. Ghost photographs have of course been published almost since the beginning of photography itself. As with psychic pictures, I can neither affirm nor assail their authenticity, for I was not present when they were taken. But in 1937 a photograph was taken under conditions no fair-minded scientist could criticize. The setting was Raynham Hall, Norfolk, England, the ancestral seat of the Marquess Townshend. As reported in *Life* of January 4, 1937, it all started innocently enough with an order to photograph the interior of the stately mansion. The firm hired to undertake this task was Indre Shira, Ltd., a London firm of Court photographers. In September of 1936 the company sent their representative, one Captain Hubert C. Provand, and an assistant out to Raynham Hall to do the job.

Three-hundred-year-old Raynham Hall is a rambling structure of some size within a 20,000-acre estate, where American servicemen were stationed during World War II. Since then the house has been closed to outsiders and, since the Townshends are not exactly afflicted with poverty, the widely practiced custom of admitting tourists for half a crown never invaded the august portals of the Hall. I found that my request to visit was vigorously denied by the owners, perhaps because they feared undue publicity. They were of course well aware of the fact that they had a ghost, but since the ghost was a direct blood relative, Lady Walpole, they did not cherish the idea of discussing her in public.

Immediately after his arrival, Captain Provand set out to work. He had no use for the supernatural, and if he had heard of the ghostly legends he put no stock into them. But one of his cameras was smashed by seemingly unseen hands. Still he refused to accept the possibility of a ghost being the culprit. At one point during their meticulous work of photographing the interior of the Hall, the two men found themselves facing the famous grand staircase in the Great Hall downstairs. "Look!" the assistant suddenly said, and pointed toward the staircase, terror etched on his face. The captain looked but saw nothing. The young man insisted he saw a white figure slowly descending the stairs. "Well," the skeptical captain replied, "if you're so sure of it, let's photograph it." Quickly they pointed their camera toward the staircase and made an exposure. This was done with flash, but one must remember that in

20. *Famed "Brown Lady of Raynham Hall" descending staircase was snapped by Capt. Provand in 1936. She is the ghost of Dorothy Walpole, who died tragically there.*

HOW THIS PICTURE WAS OBTAINED.

Time:	*September, 1936.*
Place:	*Raynham Hall, Norfolk, England.*
Light conditions:	*Daytime, flashlight.*
Camera:	*Still camera, 8 x 10.*
Exposure:	*Flash.*
Operator:	*Captain Provand of Indre Shira, Ltd.*
Developing:	*Blake, Sandford, & Blake.*

1936 flash photography was not yet what it is today, and the intensity of the flash light very much weaker than with modern flashbulbs. At this the figure dissolved—at least the assistant reported it was no longer visible to him. The two photographers then sealed the plate and took it to the chemists' firm of Blake, Sanford & Blake, where the negative was developed. The chemists attested to the fact that nothing had been wrong with either negative or developing, and that the figure on the staircase was not due to slipshod handling of any kind.

The striking figure is that of a woman in flowing dress, descending the staircase. It is white and smokelike, and the stairs can be seen through it. When the results were shown to the Townshends there was a moment of embarrassed silence. Then the photograph was compared with a portrait of Lady Dorothy Walpole which hung in one of the upstairs passages. It was also pretty much the same as the reported apparition of the lady seen by a number of Townshend house guests over the years.

What made Dorothy Walpole a ghost, way back in the 1780s, was a little inconvenience called mental depressions, but in those days this was considered a disease not fit to be discussed in polite society. Being of gentle birth, the lady was therefore "contained" in a room upstairs and spent her last years in it, finally passing across the threshold of death no longer in her right mind. Perhaps she was not aware of this change and considers Raynham Hall still her rightful home, and herself free now to range it at will, and to smash intruding photographers' cameras if she so desires.

Life published the picture with all the facts and left it to the viewer to make up his own mind. I have shown this picture on national television and before many college audiences and have never failed to get gasps from the audience, for it is indeed the very model of what a ghost picture should look like.

It occurred to me that there should be a reasonably controlled way of obtaining photographs of so-called ghosts, by simply photographing as many haunted places as possible under varying conditions and from many angles. If ghosts are two-dimensional in character, as I suspected, then of course hitting the proper angle or plane of their existence was extremely hazardous, and the chance of finding it not very great. On the other hand, I had nothing to lose by trying.

Impressed by the Raynham ghost picture (known as "the Brown Lady of Raynham Hall"), I discussed this subject with Eileen Garrett, president of Parapsychology Foundation. The Foundation had in the past sponsored me three times, giving me modest grants to carry on my work of investigating haunted houses and mediums. But somehow Mrs. Garrett at that time had no use for the subject of psychic photography, assuring me that to the best of her knowledge it was all fraudulent and not worth the effort. I found myself disagreeing with my old friend, and went on on my own with the research. My camera was to be a hand-made Zeiss, Super Ikonta B model, which is exceptionally well suited for work in dark areas, as its large lens has a high degree of light-sensitivity and its mechanical parts are precision-made. Above all, this camera has a lock that prevents accidental double exposure. In order to advance the film one has to turn the key a full 180 degrees. Only then does the mechanism snap into place. An imperfect turn will not activate the camera. This is important, as it means that only square pictures of the exact size the camera was built for can be exposed by it under normal conditions. No odd sizes, oblong pictures or other accidents of size and shape are possible. When the key has been properly turned, one must first cock the shutter fully and hear it click into place. Only then is the camera ready for work. By depressing the exposure button on top of the camera the cocked shutter is released and the picture is taken. In order to take a second picture one has to repeat the entire process. If one of the three steps is omitted the camera will not work, and double exposures cannot occur. In fact, the only way to get double exposure with this camera is to take the film out and replace it in the camera—in other words, out-and-out fraud.

Next I decided that only the fastest film would do, since any form of flashlight or strong artificial light would in my opinion destroy the sensitive psychic elements I set out to photograph. Besides, one might be accused of light reflections or refractions. I therefore decided to work only with soft light; that is, daylight or ordinary room light. The only film fast enough to give me acceptable results with so little light was the Agfa Record Isopan, a black-and-white film with very little grain that can be developed to a 1200 ASA rating, about twelve times higher than that of the average black-and-white film used by amateurs. Unfortunately there was then, when I started this experiment (1964), no really fast color film. Things have improved a little since, but not nearly enough to allow me to substitute color film on all occasions.

Now I did not deliberately set out to photograph a ghost. I never thought that would work, nor do I now think so. What I did do was take large amounts of location pictures, with as much variety of angle and timing as possible. If ghosts are electromagnetic fields impressed on the atmosphere of their demise, then they should be capable of being measured by sensitive instruments. They have been measured by Geiger counters on a number of occasions. But I wanted something visual also, and it occurred to me that psychic sensitivity was somehow related to magnetism. Could not film also record these impressions? This was pure guesswork on my part until April of 1964. Then something happened that showed me I was on the right track with this quest.

One of my longest and most difficult investigations concerned a pleasant-looking bungalow in Los Angeles, built around 1929, and owned by the present owners since the beginning. After a couple of years in the house, the owners were forced to sublease because of financial reverses, and for nine years strangers lived in the house, not all of whom can be still recalled by the owners. It was during that period of estrangement from their house that something evidently took place to leave an indelible imprint on its atmosphere. When they repossessed their home, the L.'s soon discovered that they were being plagued by a variety of psychic phenomena that frightened them. At the same time they started to make inquiries into the events that had taken place at the house in their absence.

The disturbances ranged from measured footsteps where no one was seen to walk, to raps at their door, and from the feelings of presences—there were actually two, one male and one female—to such specific and detailed occurrences as a fight to the finish taking place audibly, but not visually, in the living room over and over again, only to stop abruptly when a member of the family opened the door from one of the bedrooms. The center of ghostly manifestations seemed to have been the bedroom where Helen L., the owner's oldest daughter, slept, and the patio in the back of the house. On one occasion the noise of a struggle on the furniture-filled patio awoke all members of the family, which consisted of Helen L., her aged mother and another sister. But upon checking this out they found the furniture completely untouched. It was then that they remembered a call from their erstwhile neighbors, while the L.'s were living elsewhere, advising them that a terrible fight had taken place in their house. The neighbors had clearly heard the noise of furniture being broken. When the L.'s repossessed their house they found that the report had not been exaggerated. Broken furniture filled their house. Several witnesses confirmed hearing footsteps of someone they did not see, and Helen L. heard the sounds of someone trying to break into her bedroom through the French doors from the patio. That someone was a young girl, judging from the sound of the footsteps. The other footsteps, heard also by a number of witnesses, were heavy footfalls of a man in pursuit. In addition, the sounds of a wild party resounded in the darkness around her, and on one occasion she heard a voice telling her to get out of her own house. Naturally, Helen L. was upset at all this and asked for my help. On my first visit I made sure that she was a reasonably rational individual. I later returned in the company of the head of the Los Angeles chapter of the American Society for Psychic Research, as witness. I was also accompanied by Maxine Bell, a local psychic. Without any foreknowledge of where she was being taken by me, or an opportunity to talk to the owners of the house, Mrs. Bell clairvoyantly described the sudden violence that had erupted in this house in 1948, involving two men and a girl.

With the head of the Los Angeles chapter of the American Society for Psychic Research had come an associate, an engineer by profession, who also had psychic leanings. Separately from Mrs. Bell, he described his impressions of an older man and a very young girl, a teenager, who had died at the same time here. As I always do, I took routine location pictures all over the house with black-and-white fast film and without artificial light sources. I was quite alone in the haunted bedroom when I took six or seven exposures.

When these were later developed by the laboratory employed by Fotoshop of New York, one of them also showed a young girl in what appears to be a negligée standing at the window, looking toward the bed. The figure is solid enough, although the left flank is somewhat illuminated by the infiltrating sunshine from the patio. But on close inspection it is clear that the figure is not actually standing on the floor near the French doors, but rather *above* the floor near the bed. I examined the room again later to make sure no curtains could have been mistaken for this apparition; there were no curtains. Since the picture was taken, I made several trips back to Los Angeles to help send the two ghosts away, and much additional evidence has piled up. But essentially it was the story of a young girl with men

fighting over her. Someone seemed to have been hurt in the process. There were indications that a body might still be hidden in the garden, but to this date the owner of the house has refused to dig for it. After the L.'s had moved back into their house, they had found blood spots on the floor.

I was very much shaken up by this picture, especially as it came quite unexpectedly. None of the other exposures on the same roll showed anything significant. I felt that the presence of both Mrs. Bell and Helen L. in the immediate vicinity was responsible for the picture, as I never considered myself psychic. I should add that I have since gone back to that same house several times, and never been able to duplicate the ghost picture. This is not surprising in view of my conviction that such apparitions are two-dimensional, and there are countless planes possible within the same 360-degree area. It is perhaps a moot question whether we are dealing here with ghosts in the strict sense of the term, meaning a human personality "hung up" in time and outside space, or with a mere impression, an imprint of violence left behind by an event in the past. Either way, it is a paranormal occurrence in the sense of parapsychology, but I am inclined to consider this particular case one of a genuine ghost, inasmuch as the personality did react in various ways at various times and in general showed traits of a disturbed human personality, something a "dead" imprint just would not do.

21. *"Girl in negligee," Holzer dubbed this time exposure taken by him in Hollywood house where murder took place.*

HOW THIS PICTURE WAS OBTAINED.

Time: *April 18, 1964, 3 P.M.*

Place: *Ardmore Boulevard, Los Angeles (exact location withheld), the house of Helen L., an executive secretary going to business in Los Angeles.*

Light conditions: *Normally bright afternoon, sunny. Inside the house, windows open. The bedroom windows, actually French doors, are covered by a pair of blinds, but no other curtains of any kind. Sunlight from the garden and patio coming through French doors. No reflecting surfaces inside room, except a mirror completely outside field of vision. Bedspread opaque, carpet opaque, no artificial light.*

Camera: *Super Ikonta B, Zeiss, in excellent working condition.*

Film: *Agfa Record Isopan 120, fast black-and-white film, rated 1200 ASA.*

Exposure: *Two seconds from a firm support, camera resting on linen chest in back of bedroom. Normally, at this exposure, film should be burned completely and no image should show.*

Operator: *Hans Holzer, alone in bedroom; medium Maxine Bell and owner of house, Helen L., seated outside bedroom in adjacent living room.*

Although I was jubilant over this picture, I did not announce it to anyone; rather I continued to do a lot of investigating of haunted areas and a lot of photographing in the process.

Within a few months' time this evidence came to me quite unexpectedly. As a result of a casual visit to one of England's famous cathedrals, I was able to produce a photograph of far greater clarity than the famous "Brown Lady of Raynham Hall," until then considered the most authentic ghost picture extant.

My wife and I were on a journey to Southampton to appear there on television and then go on to Beaulieu, where I wanted to investigate hauntings at the ancient abbey. Winchester Cathedral is in direct line with this destination, and so I decided to stop over briefly at the famed cathedral. I had heard that a number of witnesses had observed ghostly monks walking in the aisles of this church, where no monks have actually walked since the 1500s. During the dissolution of the monasteries upon orders of Henry VIII, monks and abbots were abused and occasionally executed or murdered, especially when they resisted the orders driving them from their customary places. Here at Winchester, so close to the capital, the order was strictly enforced and the ghostly monks seen by a number of witnesses may indeed have had some unfinished "business"! On researching the matter, I discovered that I was not the first man to obtain psychic photographs in this place. According to a dispatch of the *Newark Evening News* of September 9, 1958, an amateur photographer by the name of T. L. Taylor was visiting the ancient cathedral with his family. Taylor, who was then forty-two years old, an electrical engineer by profession, was on a sightseeing trip as a tourist without the slightest interest in or knowledge of the supernormal. He took a number of pictures in the choir area—the same area where my ghostly monks appeared—in late 1957. With him at the time was Mrs. Taylor and his then sixteen-year-old daughter Valerie. Incidentally, none of them observed any ghostly goings-on whatever.

The first exposure turned out to be a normal view of the choir chairs, but on the following picture—perhaps taken from a slightly different angle—there appeared in these same *empty* chairs thirteen human figures dressed in what appeared to be medieval costumes. When the film and prints came back from the lab, Taylor was aghast. As a technician he knew that his camera could not take double exposures accidentally—just as mine can't—because of a locking mechanism, and the manufacturer of the film confirmed to him upon inquiry that the film was in no way faulty and the "ghosts" could not be explained through some form of error in manufacture of film or developing. Satisfied that he had somehow obtained some supernormal material, Taylor turned the results over to the Lewisham Psychic Research Society, where they presumably still are.

As soon as we had dashed from the car

through the heavy rainfall into the cathedral, Catherine and I walked up to the choir chair area and I began to take black-and-white photographs, exposing two seconds for each picture. The high content of moisture in the atmosphere may have had some bearing on the supernormal results. On other occasions I have found that moist air is a better psychic conductor than dry air. After I had exposed the entire roll of eleven pictures in various directions, but from the same area, we returned to our car, still of course totally ignorant as to whether anything unusual would show on the negatives. Since all of my psychic photography is unexpected and purely accidental, no thoughts of what might turn up filled my mind at the time. I was merely taking photographs of the cathedral because people had observed ghosts in it. Only later did I discover that someone else had also obtained photographs of ghosts there.

Upon developing and printing it became immediately clear that I had caught the cowled, hooded figures of three monks walking in the aisle. On close inspection it is clear that we are dealing here not with one identical picture of a monk exposed somehow three times as he moved about but with three slightly different figures, one of which looks sideways, while the other two are caught from the rear. I was puzzled by the apparent lack of height on the part of these figures and wondered if sixteenth-century men were that much smaller than we are. But on examination of the records I discovered that the stone floor of the cathedral was raised a hundred years after the last monks had been driven out from Winchester. Thus the figures caught here are walking on what to them must be the original floor!

Jubilant, I took these two photographs, along with other less spectacular ones, to Mrs. Garrett, at the same time showing her my camera and how it worked. She listened quietly and then admitted that perhaps there had been a breakthrough after all. She knew me well enough to know that any possibility of fraud on my part was out of the question, and the evidence before her eyes, together with the circumstances of its production, was such that no one with normal eyesight could deny they were human figures—figures that should not, and could not, appear on the negatives, but that nevertheless did do just that.

One of the most curious of all pictures ever taken by me with my camera also involved the kind of back-up proof very few psychic investigations get. The story itself concerns a house in North Stamford, owned then by Bob and Dotty Cowan, rational and intelligent individuals who make their living as art director and actress respectively. They had been living for some time in a colonial house dating back to 1780 (so they were told), but lately the uncanny noises, footsteps and other strange goings-on had been such that they decided to call for help, and I was brought in.

In the middle of February of 1964 I paid the house a visit in the company of my wife

22. *"Ghostly monks of Winchester Cathedral"*
were photographed by Hans Holzer when
he and Mrs. Holzer were alone in the
church. An amateur named Taylor also
caught the ghosts in 1958. Ghosts seem
short but floor of church was raised a hun-
dred years after Dissolution of the Monas-
teries.

HOW THIS PICTURE WAS OBTAINED.

Time: *September 15, 1964, 11* A.M.
Weather: Heavy rain.

Place: *Winchester Cathedral, Eng-*
land, main nave, area of the
choir chairs.

Light
conditions: *Overcast skies (rain) produc-*
ing flat daylight through over-
head church windows, but no
direct light, no artificial light
source of any kind, and no re-
flecting surfaces of any kind
within the area photographed.

Camera: *Super Ikonta B, Zeiss, fre-*
quently examined for faults by
the Zeiss workshop in New
York City, and found in perfect
working order.

Film: *Agfa Record Isopan 120, from*
fresh pack purchased at Foto-
shop, New York City. Camera
loaded in subdued light.

Exposure: *Two seconds with camera rest-*
ing on firm surface, i.e.,
wooden back of choir chair.
Exposures were taken at that
time in four different directions
from the same vantage point.

Operator: *Hans Holzer, in the presence of*
Mrs. Holzer. Otherwise entire
nave of church deserted.

Developing
and
printing: *Kodak of London, professional*
department.

Catherine. The story of the psychic phenomena in the house and my two visits culminating in an exorcism has been reported in *Ghosts I've Met,* my earlier book, and I will touch here only on those aspects of the case concerning themselves with psychic photography. During our first visit to the 1780 house, we were standing in a room on the main floor of the building when I clearly heard heavy footfalls overhead. My wife heard them, too, and so did the Cowans, who managed a wan, triumphant "I told you so" type of smile.

I raced up the wooden stairs to the upper floor only to find myself in the dark, literally, for the upper floor was empty and none of the lights were on. Nobody had been walking on that floor; that is, nobody of flesh and blood. Next to the room in which I had heard the ghostly footsteps was a smaller room, partitioned off from the larger room but most likely once part of the same living quarters. It was in this room that Mrs. Cowan had had a most unusual visual experience not long before. "Like lightning," she described it, "a bright light suddenly come and gone."

Now, I accept the power of suggestion, since I myself am a professional hypnotist and know all the tricks of the trade. Consequently I took very good care that the reported experience by Mrs. Cowan did not intrude on my subconscious mind. I sat there in the dark room, definitely hostile toward any similar manifestation rather than eager for it to happen to me.

Before the lights had been turned off I had made a careful search of the room and its appointments. The windows were placed in such a manner as to make any reflection of passing headlights out of the question. There was no road immediately near the house, only the dark countryside surrounding the building. I tried the stairwell lights to see if they would reflect into the room, but all they did was cast a small amount of low-intensity light into the area nearest to the door of the room.

The four of us then turned out the lights and sat down quietly, waiting for such phenomena as might honor us. A few minutes went by and the only noise we heard was the ticking of a grandfather clock. At this precise moment my eyes were fastened on the back wall of the little room. Suddenly I noticed a flash of white light in the corner opposite me. It was a bright flash, as if a photographic flashgun had just gone off. The whole phenomenon took only a moment, but Dotty Cowan also saw it and excitedly exclaimed, "There it is again—exactly as I saw it!"

After this initial experience I returned to the house with medium Ethel Johnson Meyers, without telling her anything about the case or our own experiences. During the first visit she managed to contact one of the entities in the house, and the rest on a second visit in December. Between the two visits the activities at the house increased considerably. Footsteps were heard and lights were clearly seen in the empty house by the Cowans as they approached in the evening. They heard noises not easily explained on ordinary grounds.

The gist of the two seances was a harrowing story of crime and guilt. A young girl named Lucy or Laurie was born in 1756. Her grandfather, Samuel, disapproved of a certain young man's paying attention to his granddaughter. The young man's name was Benjamin. Samuel confessed to having killed Benjamin and thrown his body down a well in 1774. A family name was also mentioned, which I took to be Harmon, although I could not hear it too clearly. Apparently the body was later taken from the well and both grandfather Samuel and young Benjamin were buried on the hill "in back of a white structure on these grounds." Moreover, the entranced medium reported, both tombstones had been mishandled by vandals and were broken off close to the earth. At the time I wrote my report on this case the 1780 house was known on record back to 1780 only, thence the name. But I said almost prophetically then—"Could not another building have occupied the area?" That was in the spring of 1965.

On November 1, 1965, the *Stamford Advocate* carried an interesting story. It appeared that the Stamford Historical Society had been doing some exploring in a house next to the 1780 house. Accidentally they came across an old well on a hill. The owners of the adjacent house had been digging up old stones, one of which turned out to be a gravestone. With the help of the Historical Society volunteers they managed to find five more fragments of gravestones. When properly cleaned, the stones turned out to be "broken off at the ground" indeed, inscribed BENJAMIN, SAMUEL and BARNUM. Also, one fragment with the date "1746" proving that the 1780 house was older than 1780, since this was once all one and the same property. Physical proof for psychic information is not always obtained in so spectacular a manner, of course, but in this case the jigsaw puzzle did indeed fall into place.

During my third visit, Ethel Johnson Meyers and I "sat" in the "ship" room in front. The trance took place in that part of the house. At one point I felt compelled to take some photographs in the existing electric room light. I aimed my camera toward a chair in which my wife Catherine was sitting, and exposed briefly, for the room was pretty well lit. Imagine my surprise when the roll was developed. To begin with, the "odd picture" on this roll—the only one with unusual characteristics—was one and a half times larger than all others, something quite incomprehensible in the case of my Zeiss camera, as I have explained earlier. Ordinarily only square pictures can be taken with it.

Secondly, a writing desk which stood *in back of me* showed up on the negative where it could only have appeared if I had used a special mirror. There was, of course, no such mirror.

Finally, there is a large burst of white light

in the center of the picture, a burst of light very similar to what we had observed upstairs a little earlier!

One of the most impressive Irish ghosts among my souvenirs is the wraith at Ross House, the residence of Major M. J. Blackwell of Chicago, prominent businessman and erstwhile army officer. The house is on Clew Bay in County Mayo, and it is exquisitely appointed and furnished in period style. The period is Regency with dashes of Georgian thrown in for good measure. These is a marvelous staircase leading up to the second story, past a large Georgian window and landing, and continuing onto the upper floor where the main bedrooms are located. The staircase is of importance to my account here, as it is here that the unusual psychic photo I am about to discuss was taken. Here, too, on the staircase the wraith of an old maid was observed, walking up and down those stairs and in the area of a second staircase long removed in the structural changes of past years. A cousin of the major's actually saw the dead maid walk into a front room in 1964. The cousin, Linda Carvel by name, described the uniform the woman wore in detail, and it matched the description of an old maidservant who had been very attached to the family. Both the major and his wife have heard footsteps and knocks at their bedroom door.

I have described the events of this particular haunting in my book *The Lively Ghosts of*

23. *Stamford, Connecticut, haunted house is site of remarkable picture, showing writing desk on left, which actually was behind camera, and white energy burst to left of Mrs. Holzer.*

HOW THIS PICTURE WAS OBTAINED.

Time: *December 15, 1964. Evening.*

Place: *Cowan house, Stamford, Connecticut.*

Light conditions: *Strong room light.*

Camera: *Super Ikonta B, 120.*

Film: *Agfa Record Isopan, 120.*

Exposure: *2.8 lens and 1/25 second.*

Operator: *Hans Holzer.*

Developing and printing: *Fotoshop, New York City.*

Ireland, but the photograph came to light only after I had written the book, one roll of film having accidentally been overlooked and developed later. I took this picture around 4 P.M. on the staircase at Ross House. I did not see or feel anything unusual at the time, but simply rested the camera lightly but firmly on the banister and exposed in several direction. Only one of these exposures shows anything unusual.

Since Sybil Leek, who was with us, did not go into trance at that time for a variety of reasons, the servant girl's ghost was not actually "laid," as the technical term calls it. So I can only assume that she is still running up and down those stairs trying her ghostly best to serve the Major and Mrs. Blackwell.

Sometimes you literally stumble across an interesting case when you least expect it. In the summer of 1966 we spent half a day in Basle on our way to the airport at Muhlhause. I suggested a visit to Basle's ancient cathedral, which neither my wife nor I had ever seen. When we arrived at the square on which the huge edifice stands, overlooking the Rhine, we found that workmen were repairing and digging in part of the nave. Apparently fresh Roman masonry had been discovered and local archeologists were trying to save what they could. The cathedral is built upon very ancient ground, and the spot has been a sacred place without interruption from very ancient times. At first it was a pagan temple and burial ground, later a Roman temple and eventually

24. *Ireland's Ross House has ghost of servant girl seen by owners, Major and Mrs. M. J. Blackwell. Holzer took this picture on staircase in haunted area.*

HOW THIS PICTURE WAS OBTAINED.

Time:	*July 28, 1966. Afternoon.*
Place:	*Ross House, County Mayo.*
Light conditions:	*Daylight, overcast day, mid-afternoon.*
Camera:	*Super Ikonta B, 120.*
Film:	*Agfa Record Isopan, 120.*
Exposure:	*Two seconds on firm surface. Lens 2.8.*
Operator:	*Hans Holzer.*
Developing and printing:	*United Camera, New York City.*

a Christian church. Much of the old stone material has been incorporated into the walls and foundations of the present-day church.

Because of its prominent position as a center of religious power, Basle Cathedral saw its share of cruelty and violence. In the Middle Ages and during the Reformation, when the religious lines of demarcation were not always tightly drawn and churches often changed faiths back and forth, Basle was in the center of the storm, being on the border of the Catholic-Protestant confrontation. This much background I knew, of course, from my historical studies at the university, but I had no knowledge of any ghosts or psychic phenomena in the cathedral.

Purely as a matter of routine, I took a number of photographs inside the huge nave. The time was about 3 P.M. and though the sun was bright outside, very little light penetrated the heavy walls. In fact, the only illumination inside the church was from small electric chandeliers and whatever daylight managed to come in through windows placed way up in the walls of the nave.

When the pictures came back from the laboratory, I found that two of them showed whitish forms for which I could not account, on the basis of what I had observed in the church. One of these two clearly shows a kind of human skeleton with a head and legs drawn up—precisely the way people were sometimes buried in the Middle Ages when space was limited, such as in the walls of churches or in

25. *Basle's ancient Cathedral picture shows luminous skeleton-like figure with legs drawn up above solid wall.*

HOW THIS PICTURE WAS OBTAINED.

Time:	*August, 1966. Midafternoon.*
Place:	*Basle Cathedral.*
Camera:	*Super Ikonta B, 120.*
Film:	*Agfa Record Isopan, 120.*
Exposure:	*Two seconds, lens 2.8. Firm surface.*
Operator:	*Hans Holzer.*
Developing and printing:	*United Camera, New York.*

catacombs. Religious dignitaries were often honored by burial within the walls of a church or monastery, but now and then heretics were punished by being buried alive. Which is the case here we may never know, but that there is no rational explanation for the "skeleton" in my photograph I am certain. Only solid wall exists in back of it, and the nearest light source is a small electric overhead lamp illuminating a tablet farther back in the nave. I took the picture with my Zeiss resting solidly on the back of a chair, which is born out by the relative sharpness of the picture showing sharply defined chair backs and columns. Only the figures in the background of my photograph are out of focus—which they should indeed be, as they were in motion, while chairs and columns were not. I wonder who the unknown ghost at Basle Cathedral really is, and one of these days I hope to find out.

Photographing a haunted place does not always yield a recognizable human figure, of course, as we will presently see. There are other forms of paranormal photography no less interesting and equally at variance with existing photographic and optical laws. But the capture on film or photographic paper of a transparent or semi-solid human figure does create a special kind of excitement when the conditions are known to be such that fraud or self-delusion are excluded. That which I do myself is of course most believable to me, but I realize that others have also taken pictures of ghosts under con-

ditions similar to those I consider satisfactory.

Dr. Andrew von Salza's encounters with psychic photography I have discussed in detail earlier. Although all of his "extras" were obtained as the result of "induced" experiments (except perhaps the first two incidents), the one I am about to relate was not in any way planned or expected, but came about as the result of pure chance, if there is such a thing.

In 1963 he had gone to vacation at the popular Northern Californian resort of Aetna Springs, near St. Helena, where a large golf course was among the attractions. Still the camera buff, he struck up an acquaintance with the resort's owner, one George Heibel. It seemed that Heibel had a stereo camera, which then was the latest in unusual photographic equipment, although they are now a bit passé. A stereo camera gives an "in-depth" view of a scene, which is due to its taking two pictures simultaneously. This was a Wollensack, and the two men decided to try for some good shots on the golf course. It was midafternoon on a sunny day in the late summer, so they set the lens at F/16, and exposed 1/250 of a second, using daytime color film with a rating of 160 ASA. After taking a number of shots, Heibel, it appeared, allowed von Salza to use the camera and take two more pictures. What they saw was just a golf course, the area in which they were standing being empty. When the film came back from the laboratory they were in for a big surprise, for although most of the

roll showed just the golf course, the two pictures taken by von Salza with Heibel's camera
were quite different.

Two different views of a group of robed
monks appeared seemingly out of nowhere,
perhaps eight or ten figures in all, and on one
of the pictures surrounded by what appeared
to be flames. One can clearly see the lighted
candles they carry in their hands, and the expression of grim determination upon their
faces. The white robes seemed to indicate that
these men were of the Dominican order. As
I reported in my book *Ghosts of the Golden
West,* I was able to bring British medium Sybil
Leek to this area in 1966, and through deep
trance establish the dramatic narrative of these
monks. Later, I corroborated the account
through research, showing that these were the
ghosts of sixteenth-century dissidents who
had defended the rights of native Indians
against the ruling Church, and had therefore
been condemned and burned.

These photographs, however, are the first
and only psychic stereo pictures taken, and one
can only marvel at the clarity and frightening
realism with which the tormented souls of the
monks have manifested themselves on film.
When Heibel saw the pictures he wanted no
part of the whole story. It upset him to such
a degree that he gave Dr. von Salza his valuable stereo camera as a gift.

On subsequent visits the doctor tried in vain
to draw Heibel into conversation about the

HOW THE FOLLOWING PICTURES WERE
OBTAINED.

Time:	*Late summer of 1963. Afternoon.*
Place:	*The golf course at Aetna Springs, St. Helena, California.*
Light conditions:	*Bright, sunny afternoon.*
Camera:	*Wollensack stereo camera.*
Film:	*Color stereo film, daytime, 160 ASA.*
Exposure:	*1/250 second at F/16.*
Operator:	*Dr. Andrew von Salza, with Mr. Heibel's camera.*
Developing:	*San Francisco photography shop.*

26. 27. *Dr. Andrew von Salza photographed golf course at Aetna Springs, California, with stereo camera but caught group of monks with candles, apparently being en-* *veloped in flames. Later research established that monks lived there briefly centuries ago.*

incident with the monks. Finally he learned from a local parish priest that monks had come to this area in the distant past even though there were no missions established here. The friars, it would seem, stayed "only a short time" and then disappeared—for unknown reasons. I received a final note concerning the transparent monks of Aetna Springs in September of 1966. Von Salza had again gone back to his favorite holiday resort only to discover that the golf course was being torn up. Evidently the place was being remodeled. Still unyielding on the subject, the owner refused to discuss it. But as my expedition in 1966 resulted in a direct contact with the monks, I am quite sure they are no longer earthbound there anyway.

Psychic Photography in Churches

Although I have shown that those hauntings which happen to occur in a church may as easily become the subject of a psychic photograph as hauntings which occur in any house or place, there seems to be still another kind of phenomenon connected with a house of worship.

When large numbers of people gather within close confines they generate body heat, which in itself is a form of energy. But religious fervor, prayer, incantations and strong desires are all forms of thought projections—that is, the actual sending out of small particles of energy from the individual mind, each particle "charged," as it were, with a mission. Many, if not all, the thought projections of a community within a church or temple have parallel thought directions, i.e., desire for divine intercession on their behalf of one kind or another. This "calling forth" of intercession may well create an electromagnetic field within the church, aided in its continuing consistency by the thick walls, the high degree of moisture usually present in churches (especially in Britain and Ireland) and the darkness prevailing in the edifice.

A number of persons totally disinterested in psychic research and completely unknown to one another or to me, until they contacted me, have had strange experiences in churches when they took random snapshots, both in color and black-and-white. I have examined the results carefully and found a similarity between the pictures that is beyond the so-called "coincidence rate." One of the cathedrals singled out for this kind of attention is Salisbury Cathedral, England. A number of people have had psychic experiences in the majestic church. Barry Bingham, editor and publisher of the *Louisville Courier-Journal,* a distinguished journalist, had an experience bordering on reincarnation and *déjà vu* when he first visited the cathedral. He had previously had a dream experience in which he had seen the church in great detail, but at an earlier age, or so it seemed to him. As a matter of record, he had never been to Salisbury, but one of his ancestors was a bishop there, and Bingham discovered the other Bingham's tomb on his very first visit to the ancient church!

Mrs. Karl F. Wihtol is the wife of the president of Wihtol Industries, manufacturers of industrial and laboratory equipment, in New Jersey. She is also an avid amateur photographer and travels quite a bit. On Saturday, July 28, 1962, she found herself at Salisbury Cathedral. The Bournemouth Symphony Orchestra was just rehearsing for a concert of religious music. The musicians were grouped near the altar and there were a few spectators seated in the nave. The time was four in the afternoon and the light was not too bright. Mrs. Wihtol used a stereo Realist camera, with 3-D effects, then very popular with photography buffs. Unfortunately, she had to use time exposure without putting the camera down on a firm surface, so the result is not sharp. What is a mystery, however, is the additional material which appears in sharp focus on the two negatives, while the rest of the picture is completely out of focus. In a maze of whitish substance—not as dense as the "cotton" of the seance photographs earlier discussed—there appears to be what Marjorie Wihtol calls "spaghetti"— curved, twisting rods of ectoplasm. Mrs. Wihtol saw nothing special in the church at the time. She also took black-and-white pictures with her Rolleiflex camera, but they showed nothing special either.

The 3-D slide, especially when viewed in stereo, shows the ectoplastic formation rather spectacularly. At first, when Mrs. Wihtol tried to reason it out, she suspected something was wrong with her camera or film. She took the slide to a meeting of her camera club where one of the members, an instructor in photography at nearby Fort Monmouth, wondered if a light leak had occurred. Although both stereo negatives had the same "extra," they were 3 inches apart in the camera. Also, none of the neighboring negatives in the roll showed any signs of leakage. Mrs. Wihtol sent the slide on to Eastman Kodak at Rochester, New York, and again stumped the experts. She then submitted the curious pictures to the photography experts at *Life* magazine, where no one could come up with a satisfactory explanation of the strange phenomenon. Finally she sent them to me, and I made sure that there had been no double exposure. Her camera does not permit

28. *Mrs. Marjorie Wihtol's stereo picture of Salisbury Cathedral, England, reveals ectoplastic formations, possibly letters W.R.*

HOW THIS PICTURE WAS OBTAINED.

Time: *Saturday, July 28, 1962, 4 P.M.*

Place: *Salisbury Cathedral, England.*

Light conditions: *Available daylight only.*

Camera: *Stereo Realist.*

Film: *Kodak slides, 3-D.*

Exposure: *Time exposure, hand-held camera.*

Operator: *Mrs. Karl Wihtol, Middletown, New Jersey.*

Developing: *Local, via Kodak.*

accidental slip-ups of that kind. That's where matters stood in June of 1965, when I first examined the slide.

My suggestion as to the meaning of the curious "extra" may at first sound farfetched, but it is based on observation of this type of extra obtained elsewhere, such as with Betty Ritter in New York. To my mind the crudely drawn extra represents an attempt at a monogram, with the letter W on the left and, more faintly, an R on the right. Using the available ectoplasm raised from the combination of spectators, musicians and sound energies released by the music, the intelligent entity "writing" with this raw material wanted to record his name for some unknown reason. Evidently aware of the presence of a modern recording device— and this is of course speculation on my part— the unknown "writer" painted the letters W R into the soft ectoplastic mass, very much like a finger-painting done in sand or clay.

The W is definitely an early medieval form of this initial, not the customary printed W but the much less known "cursive" form of it. Most people do not realize that even the ancient Greeks and Romans used a flowing hand, that is, a "cursive" writing, for everyday use. Monuments and official documents show us the block or printed form of the alphabet by contrast and it is that form of the alphabet we customarily refer to. During the Middle Ages sharp, unyielding pens were used to write on parchment. Consequently, the letters had to adapt themselves to the medium on which they were

29. Jesse Joseph's color picture taken of Westminster Cathedral stained glass window also revealed ectoplastic material including some jumbled letters.

HOW THIS PICTURE WAS OBTAINED.

Time:	*April 23, 1966. Noon.*
Place:	*Westminster Cathedral, London.*
Light conditions:	*Available daylight. Rainy day.*
Camera:	*Airespenta single-lens reflex.*
Film:	*Kodachrome, 35mm.*
Exposure:	*1/2 second, F/3.5.*
Operator:	*Jesse Joseph, of New York.*
Developing:	*Local shop, via Kodak.*

placed, and a flowing hand developed naturally.

There remains only one more speculation—guesswork until such time as I can establish through trance that there is indeed a psychic presence at Salisbury Cathedral—speculation as to who W R is or was. The cathedral goes back to the eleventh century or beyond. William the Conqueror was one of the rulers of England very closely connected with the cathedral. William usually styled himself WIL-LIELMUS REX rather than the expected GUGLIEL-MUS, a later development. On the coins of the period he is usually styled with a W or sometimes even a P, but never a G. Of course we may be dealing here with a different person whose initials are also W.R. But the W does belong to William the Conqueror's period, and the thought is tempting.

Not so spectacular, but equally interesting, is a photograph obtained by Jesse Joseph of New York at Westminster Abbey, London, on April 23, 1966. Mr. Joseph took two pictures with an Airespenta camera, which is a single reflex model using 35mm Kodachrome film, and no flash. It was noon, and raining outside. Mr. Joseph saw nothing special at the moment, nor did he harbor any interest in the psychic or expect that his camera might turn up some unusual "extras." In fact the entire subject was alien to him, and his pictures were brought to my attention by his brother Reuben Joseph, who saw me on television.

The slide taken of one of the stained-glass windows (which looked completely "normal" to Mr. Joseph) shows a large amount of what Mrs. Wihtol had called "spaghetti" between window and camera lens. Again the similarity is evident between this type of ectoplastic rod in the Wihtol picture and some of Betty Ritter's work. Several letters seem to be contained in the jumble of material. In the left margin area the letter Y appears quite clearly, and below it a medieval A and farther down an O, with the characteristic Gothic formation due to the inability of monks' pens to do perfect circles. In the lower right area I seemed to read a Gothic B. On turning the picture upside down, an F becomes evident, superimposed in the area of the stained-glass window's cross. There is a great deal of writing here, most of it undecipherable. Looking at the picture right side up again, I was also struck by the outline of a Bishop's mitre in the lower right area.

While this may not be a clear-cut message in the sense a trance investigation often is, it does point the way toward a new and exciting area of scientific inquiry with the color camera as tool.

Optical Reflections in Psychically Active Areas

Not every manifestation of psychic fields in haunted or otherwise psychically active areas leads to full apparitions. Sometimes the energies present are not strong enough to manifest an entire personality, or the phenomenon belongs to that shadowy category of psychic impressions left behind by a traumatic event in the past, without the continuing presence of an actual personality. I have found on a reasonably large number of occasions that such fields do exist and that they can be photographed.

Not long ago *Life* magazine published photographs of rooms taken some time after people had left them. Yet the photographs showed the figures of these persons as if they were still present. The impressions are shallow and not sharp, but they are undoubtedly those of people. *Life's* photographs were produced throught heat-sensitive cameras, not psychically. But there is a relationship between the heat imprint and the psychic imprint, inasmuch as both are energy patterns impressed on the atmosphere of an area.

I never searched for the electromagnetic fields I feel are present in the areas of emotional turmoil in a house or other enclosure, since I could not very well pinpoint them, dealing as I was with two-dimensional matters in a three-dimensional area. But by pointing my camera in as many directions as possible I greatly increased the possibility of accidentally hitting the right plane. Theoretically, of course, I could take an unlimited number of pictures in such a room, moving my camera angle ever so slightly, and then I would certainly have to include the haunted area. But practically speaking, this is a monumental task for which I am presently neither equipped nor sufficiently supported financially.

In the following pages I will present some extraordinary takes, all of my authorship, all with the same camera and type of film. What these pictures have in common are "multiple exposure" type areas that aren't multiple exposures. In every case, double exposure was impossible, film was fresh and unspoiled, developing and printing the work of experts, and the Zeiss camera had been checked within a year for possible light leaks and damage. Nothing was found.

The first picture was taken at St. Mark's-in-the-Bowerie church in New York City. It was number two on a roll of eleven exposures. None of the other nine exposures shows anything unusual; all were pictures of the church interior. But number two clearly shows multiple exposure patterns. The effect seems to be similar to a picture taken with a large mirror present in the area, to reflect part of the room. There was of course no such mirror in the church when I took the pictures. But it may well be that the psychically active area *acted* like a mirror to create the unusual distortions seen here. Although most of the details of the picture are seen twice, there appear in the upper third, center, a white dot and line not duplicated nearby or elsewhere in the photograph. They look like the ectoplasm rods shown in the previous chapter. The picture was taken in the heart of the haunted area, near a pew where a ghost had been observed.

The next series of pictures was taken during a seance in June Havoc's old town house in New York. Sybil Leek was the medium, and she is seen in the picture standing in the back of the downstairs living room, which was the center of poltergeist activities. I have told the story of this remarkable haunting in *Yankee Ghosts*, including the trance session in which a ghostly presence spoke through Sybil Leek, identifying herself under my prodding as one Lucy Ryan, a camp follower in the year 1792, whose soldier served in a regiment commanded by a certain Napier. The next day I was able to identify the commander as Col. George Napier and confirm much of the wraith's story. While we were preparing for the trance portion of our investigation, Sybil Leek stood idly by, admiring Miss Havoc's furniture and bric-a-brac. It was at this point that I started to take photos from the area of the "outer" half of the large living room, pointing my Zeiss camera toward the right rear, where most of the disturbances had taken place.

In the first picture one can see the floor boards as plain, roughly hewn Victorian wood; the wall to the right is covered with bric-a-brac and there is no obstruction whatever between

30. Hans Holzer took this multi-exposure-effect picture with one exposure at New York's haunted St. Mark's-in-the-Bowerie church.

HOW THIS PICTURE WAS OBTAINED.

Time: *March 15, 1960. Afternoon.*

Place: *St. Mark's-in-the-Bowerie church, New York City.*

Light conditions: *Available daylight, pretty dim.*

Camera: *Super Ikonta B, 120.*

Film: *Agfa Record Isopan, 120.*

Exposure: *Two seconds, on firm surface.*

Operator: *Hans Holzer; also present, mediumistic Mary M.*

Developing and printing: *United Camera, New York.*

viewer and wall. Picture number two was taken about ten minutes later, after we had all sat down. My wife Catherine is seen on the left. The floor boards now look transparent, although there was and is no way in which they could be made to reflect in this manner. Furthermore, the wall on the right is now blocked from full view by a black, irregular shape. Nothing within the camera bellows could account for this obstruction, nor can film or print be blamed for the sudden appearance of this black area.

Ten minutes later, another exposure was made after Mrs. Leek had gotten up again and stood on the exact spot where I had earlier (before her arrival) heard the poltergeist noises myself. This time the arrangement of the room shows a marked change. To begin with, my wife's knees seem cut off by a spreading reflection of the floor, as if ice or a mirror were covering the wooden boards. If this were a true, optical reflection, however, everything would have to appear *in proportion*. But this is not the case with this phenomenon. The back of the chair behind my wife does "reflect" in the floor surface, yet her knees, so much closer to the floor, do not show at all. The figure of Mrs. Leek appears strangely foreshortened. A streak of light, not accounted for by any form of leakage from the tightly packed roll of film, appears bottom right. And the black amorphous shape has now changed contours considerably. While it extends farther to the right,

31. a. Medium Sybil Leek inspects actress June Havoc's New York town house preparatory to seance. Note opaque and non-reflecting floorboards, and bric-a-brac on wall clearly visible.

HOW THESE PICTURES WERE OBTAINED.

Time: *October, 1964. Evening.*

Place: *June Havoc's town house, New York City.*

Light conditions: *Very bright electric room lights, no flash.*

Camera: *Zeiss Super Ikonta B, 120.*

Film: *Agfa Record Isopan, 120.*

Exposure: *1/25 second at F/2.8.*

Operator: *Hans Holzer.*

Developing and printing: *Fotoshop, New York.*

b. Floor begins to become transparent, black object partially obstructs view on right.

c. Floor now totally transparent, but Mrs. Holzer's knees are not reflecting, while chair in back of her is; shape on right has changed contours.

b.

c.

it seems to open up again in the lower center, permitting one to see the wall decoration behind it, which picture two did not reveal. These pictures were part of two rolls of eleven exposures each, but none of the others showed anything along these lines. All exposures were 1/25 second, since the room was quite brightly lit with artificial light.

I took the next two photographs in 1966 in Carlingford, Ireland, on the grounds of a haunted rectory we had gone to investigate. In the first photograph the owner, painter Ernest McDowell, is shown standing near his entrance gate on the very spot where he had earlier observed the ghosts of a clergyman and a girl in a red velvet dress pursuing each other. The story itself has been reported in my book *The Lively Ghosts of Ireland,* but the picture is of interest because it shows a light streak on the right that should not be there. I have other such pictures, showing similar light streaks (or energy concentrations, perhaps) that are unusual in the sense that only one or two of an entire roll would show them, and not the rest of the exposures. Now if an entire roll is fogged or accidentally light-flashed, this should show on all of the exposures. Selective light streaks do not occur. There is nothing in the developing of either film or print that could account for it, either.

The second Irish picture is even more bizarre. It was taken by my wife with my camera in one of the upstairs bedrooms. This particu-

32. Ernest McDowell standing on spot where he saw ghosts, while light rod on right appears in picture.

HOW THESE PICTURES WERE OBTAINED.

Time:	*July, 1966, afternoon.*
Place:	*Carlingford Rectory, Ireland.*
Light conditions:	*Medium clear afternoon.*
Camera:	*Super Ikonta B, 120.*
Film:	*Agfa Record Isopan, 120, furnished by German newspaperman Peter Rober of* Constanze *magazine.*
Exposure:	*1/25 second at F/2.8.*
Operator:	*Hans and Catherine Holzer.*
Developing and printing:	*Peter Rober, Hamburg.*

33. *Mrs. Catherine Holzer took this picture of haunted room at McDowell's Carlingford Rectory, Ireland. Door on left was clearly* closed *when the Holzers were in the room.*

lar room was the scene of an experience of the daughter of a former owner, a rector, now a canon, by the name of Meissner. Helen Meissner had seen the door of this room open, slowly, and then close again, by itself. Not the usual thing for doors to do, even old ones. When we visited this room in the afternoon of a July day in 1966, both Catherine and I commented on the rather run-down state of the room, and on the fact that the door on the left, leading to the next room, was firmly closed. We took some pictures, and on the one Catherine took the door appears *ajar*.

No mistake about it, the door we had seen flush with the wall, shut tight, was anything but shut when the picture was developed. The film had been exposed under the watchful eye of German newspaperman Peter Rober, who had accompanied us for a story for a Hamburg magazine and who acted as control in my psychic-photography activities on this occasion. It was his film and his developing and printing services, and I was handed the finished product afterward.

The following photograph is another one of those impossibilities in many ways. To begin with, note its odd size. As I have said, my camera is incapable, normally, of producing anything but square pictures, separated from each other by regular strips of dark film. Nothing mechanical can induce the camera to produce oblong pictures. I couldn't do it if I wanted to. Nevertheless we have here an image of more than twice the normal size; moreover, the separating strips are missing.

The story behind this picture is reported in *Ghosts of the Golden West,* although the site is actually the great castle at Steyersberg, in Austria. But the gentleman whose portrait so strangely appears on this photograph, a friend of mine by the name of Count Degenhard von Wurmbrand, had a second residence in Los Angeles, and it is there that we originally met. It is also one of the strangest cases of the already unusual world of ESP I've ever come across, involving, as it does, an ancient family curse that seemed to work. The beginning of the curse dates back to the seventeenth century, when the count's remote ancestors condemned an innocent man to death in the dungeon below the castle. His restless spirit is behind the curse, it would seem, having taken its vengeance by laying a curse on all male members of the Wurmbrand family. They were to die unnaturally, and never be happy with their wives.

Strange as it may seem, this held true for all of them, including my friend Degenhard, although his connection with the original Wurmbrand was very distant. His second marriage seemed happy, and his health was fine when I visited him in the castle in Austria. But shortly after my leaving him, with the promise of returning soon with a competent trance medium to break the curse, he died suddenly under circumstances fully bearing out the family curse. Now there is no longer a male heir bearing the name and, hopefully, the ghost is satisfied.

Our visit to Steyersberg took place in August of 1965, and while my wife was having a chat with the count's sister I accompanied him into that part of the big castle which was haunted by the seventeenth-century victim of an ancestral error of judgment. We sat down in a beautifully appointed room overlooking the majestic Styrian woods. This room, now carefully carpeted wall to wall and exquisitely furnished with antiques, served many years ago as the nursery for the young count and his brother, and it was here that a psychic experience took place at that time. The room is directly above the dungeon, which is now walled up. Because it was in the count's view the epicenter of uncanny activities, we repaired there to talk about the strange events at Steyersberg.

After the talk with Count Wurmbrand I took some photographs of him in a chair near the window. He was gay and rather youthful-looking for his age, which was about seventy, and no inkling of impending tragedy appeared on his face. Yet when the picture was developed it shows him looking rather different from how he appeared to me at the time. Aged considerably and very tired, with a face bathed in white and eyes half closed, he seemed a man at the door of death. This was in August, and in November the prediction came true. The photograph also shows portions of the room not in the line of direct vision, as far as the lens is concerned.

34. Count Degenhard von Wurmbrand in the haunted room at Steyersberg castle photographed by Hans Holzer. Note unusual shape of negative and dead-mask-like exexpression of Count, who fought century-old curse unsuccessfully.

HOW THIS PICTURE WAS OBTAINED.

Time: August, 1965.

Place: Steyersberg Castle, Austria.

Light conditions: Late afternoon, daylight only, rainy day.

Camera: Super Ikonta B, 120.

Film: Agfa Record Isopan, 120.

Exposure: Firm surface, 2 seconds. F/2.8.

Operator: Hans Holzer.

Developing and printing: United Camera, New York.

It is similar to the one taken by me at St. Mark's-in-the-Bowerie in this respect. The white material to the left of the count's right hand, which rests on his knee, is unexplained even in terms of parallel impressions of the same scene. A strange case, a strange picture.

Now we jump from a seventeenth-century castle in Austria to a twentieth-century trailer camp in Massachusetts, proving once again that psychic phenomena know neither boundaries nor time. The scene is outside Boston, where Rita Atlanta—her professional name as an exotic dancer in nightclubs—lives with her son whenever she is in America. She works part of the year in Europe, and it was in Frankfurt that we originally met. This was in the summer of 1966, and I met her again at the trailer in the winter of that year. Her experience involved seeing the ghostly apparition of a man in her camp, always at the same hour of the morning. I established first of all that she had had psychic experiences long before, and that a man had been run over by a car near the trailer Miss Atlanta called home.

On my visit in November of 1966, I took a number of photographs in Miss Atlanta's presence. This was in the afternoon, and the day was not very bright. In the area between kitchen and dining alcove where she had seen and felt the presence, several of the exposures showed a significant mirage effect similar to the transparent floor in June Havoc's house, seen earlier.

35. a. Exotic dancer Rita Atlanta in front of her haunted trailer near Boston.

HOW PICTURE 35B WAS OBTAINED.

Time:	*November, 1966.*
Place:	*Trailer camp near Boston.*
Light conditions:	*Daylight, late afternoon.*
Camera:	*Super Ikonta B, 120.*
Film:	*Agfa Record Isopan, 120.*
Exposure:	*Firm surface, 2 seconds.*
Operator:	*Hans Holzer, in presence of Rita Atlanta.*
Developing and printing:	*United Camera, New York.*

b. Table covered with ordinary tablecloth turns into reflecting surface in haunted area in this Hans Holzer picture.

The first picture shows Miss Rita Atlanta in front of her trailer, an example of how unromantic some haunted houses can look. The trailer is only a few years old and was bought new.

The second, a picture of the dining-room table inside the trailer, shows the reflection effect quite plainly. This is remarkable, as it was covered with a nonreflecting tablecloth and there was no mirror or other reflecting surface nearby that could have been blamed for this phenomenon. As usual, great care was taken to make sure that neither camera nor film had any light leaks or accidental exposures.

Psychic Photography—Threshold of a New Science?

The word *science,* to begin with, means a state of knowing, from the Latin word *scire,* to know. It does not mean, as so many modern practitioners think, the only *proper* way to knowledge. There are other paths, just as effective and sometimes more accurate than the scientific road. One cannot supply concrete proof of mystic identification with other beings as we understand the term, but, to the experimenter, the experience itself is infinitely more accurate and direct than any scientific attempt to interpret it for him. Still, insofar as is possible, I am committed to the scientific approach to psychic phenomena: I will always present factual information before drawing any personal conclusions about it. Scientists in most fields disagree in their interpretation of fact, to the advantage of progress, I think, but they don't or should not disagree as to *what* these facts are.

This is where parapsychology is a difficult field, for it cannot stand upon the accumulated evidence of repeatable laboratory experiment *alone,* if at all. Neither, for that matter, can oceanography or the study of volcanoes and earthquakes. They depend on qualified observation and evaluation *as well,* and it is this kind of parapsychology that I am speaking of.

There is no doubt in my mind that qualified observation is as scientific as re-creation under artificial conditions, if not more so. This is particularly true in this field where emotional factors are at the bottom of the phenomena, and where environmental influences are also significant. A psychic person fully relaxed in my living room will perform a lot better after some low-pressure chatting than a medium placed in a sterile cubicle in a laboratory, with the cold, uncommitted eyes of the researcher demanding results then and there. I am a researcher and I am not uncommitted. I have had significant evidence that psychic phenomena exist; my job now is to study them *further* and to learn more about them. The subject feels this and performs accordingly.

The use of subjective material, no matter how carefully screened and how well documented, still requires a basis of acceptance that the people involved—researcher and subject—are not fraudulently involved in reporting the results. Not very likely, I admit, but then some scientists, disturbed by the implications of a survival view in science, will go to great extremes to discredit that which they cannot swallow even if it is true.

I have found the camera a faithful servant, demanding neither emotional attachment nor loyalty on my part. The lens, often more sensitive than the human eye, will perform if its mechanical components are intact, and it does not manufacture anything of its own volition. Cameras and film are objective proof that what they deliver is true, provided the mechanical components are in proper shape.

Dr. Jule Eisenbud and Ted Serios have

shown that men's thoughts can be put down on sensitive film at will, in what are close to controlled laboratory experiments. My own work leads the way into spontaneous field work along the same lines, while at the same time it pierces the barriers of time and space as we know them. The implications of such photography, when one realizes that fraud is impossible, are that man possesses something more than a flesh-and-blood machine called the body. It follows, therefore, that there must be some other place or state of existence where that part of man continues his being.

At the same time, I have pointed out—I am not the first one to do so, I am sure—that man's personality or soul, if you prefer, is also, in its strictest sense, an electromagnetic energy field, and as such is capable of registering on certain instruments, some already in existence, some as yet to be built. Photographic film and paper are among the tools by which man can prove his nonphysical component.

It is perhaps a pity that we find it so difficult to supply the funds to establish, equip and staff an institute where psychic research is the only subject studied, where no theory is considered too far off the mark to be worthy of examination, and where scientists of every conceivable kind, persuasion and background can work hand in hand toward the greatest of all remaining "last frontiers": inner space, man himself!

About the Author

Hans Holzer has long specialized in the study and interpretation of parapsychology phenomena. He has written many books on the subject and frequently lectures and appears on television.

Mr. Holzer was educated at Vienna and Columbia Universities, where he studied archaeology and history.